Buddhism and Computing

How to Flourish in the Age of Algorithms

Paul Trafford

MUD PIE

Mud Pie Books
Oxford OX2 6HY
Registered Co. No.4405635

ISBN 978-1-912952-02-1

www.mudpiebooks.com

MUD
PIE

In memory of David S. S. Yau

Contents

Prologue

MINDFULNESS. BREATHE IN, knowing that you are breathing in; breathe out, knowing that you are breathing out. Simple and easeful, it is quintessential Buddhist practice. So what does it have to do with computing and machines crunching through complex calculations using sophisticated algorithms? What benefit might there be in drawing them together?

Computing is a science. Buddhism is a religion. Yet it is often claimed that there is a close affinity, especially in the expression of interdependence and process. Researchers have identified links with neuroscience, quantum mechanics, artificial intelligence and other emerging fields of science. But are these analyses really *Buddhist*? And are these endeavours really ennobling humanity?

As a practising Buddhist who has worked in computing and IT I have been exploring such connections for some while. Delving into my personal memory banks, I recall the first computer science lecture I attended, in October 1987, which started with the following words handwritten on the blackboard:

Insight - not numbers.

It is in that spirit that I see the need, greater than ever, to write about humanity and software systems, especially with regard to social networking. I have long felt that the ethical aspects of online behaviour have been neglected, so in my investigations I have promoted them to become the main perspective. In doing so it soon becomes evident that one topic needs special attention: artificial intelligence (AI). To explore this properly I have had to step back and consider fundamental questions concerning what it means to be human and what are the properties of mind. This has led me to settle on the very general title, *Buddhism and Computing*. I hope the linkage will make sense as the chapters unfold.

One might reasonably object that there were no computers in existence at the time of the Buddha, so what relevance could his teachings have for computing? Well, it depends on what you mean by 'compute'! The Latin verb, *computāre*, means 'to count, sum up, reckon together'. Humans can count, figure things out and so on. We are in this sense 'computers', but our usual notions are of machines made from silicon and metal, distinct from humans, even if our interactions are becoming closer and more frequent.

This proximity is especially evoked by the third term, which speaks to what's happening right now – computing has moved into the age of reckoning, as it were, with an array of diverse applications ranging from weather forecasting to medical diagnosis and from genomics to online social media feeds. One cannot fail to notice that articles on AI and machine learning are featuring prominently and with increased regularity in the mass media and popular debate. But is it really wise to trust software with such important decision-making? The implications for human beings and being human are not distant, they are already affecting us in significant ways.

Much of the research and development has been driven by the question: Can machines exhibit human-like intelligence? Many investigations have focused on this from the technical perspective of the machine, ignoring the broader ramifications for humanity. Seeking to address this lacuna, we ask: What should we make of this phenomenon and our relationship to it? What are the ethical implications?

This is where the linkage with Buddhism can be made with reference to its texts and traditions. I can't provide comprehensive answers or complete solutions here, but I can offer a fresh orientation. As a human being and a spiritual guide, the Buddha roused his followers to practice a path for achieving well-being in daily life. We can apply this ethical approach in our examination of some fundamental aspects and popular developments in computing, whose evaluation may be simply expressed in human terms: Does it aid or hinder our progress on this path?

This small volume is not intended as a general guide to Buddhism. It is more a comparative investigation into notions of computation, what it means to think, and the potential impact of algorithms and AI on matters of human agency, all of which I seek to bring together by applying Buddhist approaches to the design of computing systems. Some language is unavoidably technical, but it is otherwise largely informal, drawing on a broad range of subject areas, not just mathematics and Buddhist texts. Whilst the expressions may be novel, the underlying ideas and practice have been around for a *long* time and have ancient roots – though it is all too easy to forget them.

1

Numbers and Computation

A discomfiting challenge

ONE SUMMER'S DAY in 1984 my family visited Freda Wint, a long-standing Buddhist friend of my mother who lived in Oxford.[1] We met up for lunch and then repaired to Freda's home to sit outside in the garden. I found myself a comfy chair and prepared to settle down, but Freda turned to me and asked a question that shook me from my imminent reverie: 'Does mathematics exist as an external reality or is it a fabrication of the mind?' I was fifteen years old and a bit dumbfounded at first (it wasn't the kind of question they asked at school). After a pause, I hesitantly suggested that, because of the symmetry inherent in nature, there *was* mathematics to be discovered 'out there'. 'Mystical!' came back the response. Seeing her puzzled expression, a sense of unease befell me.

I soon learnt that few people who met Freda got

off lightly, as she had a habit of using questions to probe the nature of mind in its deepest sense. She epitomised the spirit of human enquiry, engaged in the search for meaning.

Although at the time I wasn't aware of it, this question has often been asked down the ages. It was especially topical a century or more ago, when a certain Indian mathematician arrived in Cambridge. More on him shortly ...

Fast forward a couple of years and I was scanning shelves in the reference section of Birmingham Central Library for a school project. I came across a book on the logical foundations of computer science. It was not what I was looking for, but I picked it up out of curiosity. Prior to that moment, my exposure had been mainly through writing code on a Sinclair ZX Spectrum and I naively thought of computing as something entirely practical. So I was amazed to see rows and rows of dense mathematical notation with impenetrable equations – a completely foreign language that looked very forbidding.

I remained in the dark until subsequently carrying out some university research in computer science, where I learnt that the formal foundations are indeed mathematical. Yet somehow the nature of the reasoning *felt* different to me; it still seemed alien to pure mathematics undertaken for its own sake. Perhaps it had to do with the distinct mental activities involved. To try and elucidate this it is helpful to consider something basic to both: numbers. For numbers can be abstract or concrete, and how we come to consider them takes us deep into the nature of mind.

Returning to Freda's question, I want to approach it by reflecting especially on whole numbers. These are zero, 1, 2, 3, etc., and their negative counterparts, −1, −2, −3, etc. My own familiarity with numbers was instilled early on as a child in nursery school when I was taught to count and then do basic arithmetic, aided by drill recital of times tables. At the same time I discovered a liking for jigsaws, which are a wonderful means of developing a sense of order and composition in a whole formed of distinct but related parts.

A few years later, I touched on infinite series for the first time through a 'number spider'. The teacher gave us a whole number to put at the centre, the spider's body. We then had to think of expressions that equated to that number. We would write each such expression somewhere on the sheet of paper and then draw a spider's leg from the central body to the expression – the more legs the better. I soon realised that I could iterate: if 10, say, were the central number, I could write 1 + 9 for the first leg, and then 2 + 8 for the second, and so on, until 10 + 0, 11 − 1, 12 − 2, etc., but I would scatter these legs around the sheet so that the teacher wouldn't see what I was up to!

These examples illustrate basic but powerful skills of human computation and hint at an underlying ability to *represent* much bigger numbers. If we were to keep on counting, we could in theory reach a number that exceeds the number of atoms in the universe. So, although they can't be written down directly, we can still represent them and reason with them.

Here's a silly game for two people to illustrate representation (Advice: don't play it with a mathematician!). It is called the 'higher number game' and it's quite straightforward. Two people independently think of a number and the one who picks the higher number wins. Naturally, people choose a positive real number, so you can decide beforehand to choose a symbolic number, $N + 1/N$ where N represents your opponent's number. This number will usually be just a tiny bit bigger. This example, although trivial, also illustrates an innate human capacity to see what's there and then go beyond.

Recreation aside, how fundamental is mathematics to our thinking? There is growing evidence from neurological studies that mathematical ability is inherent and occurs long before language skills. Experiments conducted by Brian Butterworth using eye-tracking of infants appear to show significant indications that – even during their first week – they can discriminate between differing numbers of objects.[2] In mathematical jargon, they understand *cardinality*.

Where does this mathematical ability come from? As a neuroscientist, Professor Butterworth's work involves identifying and physically measuring the activation of specific regions in the brain relating to designated activities. This kind of analysis is useful for diagnosis of medical conditions. With a sufficient body of evidence, we know to associate certain neural activities with certain kinds of mental processing – hence the term 'neural correlates'. Correlations are not, however, sufficient to demonstrate *causes*; to establish these, we are going to investigate the mind from a different perspective.

Mathematics and intuition

Let us develop our exploration of the subtleties of mind and numbers with the seventeenth-century French philosopher and mathematician, Blaise Pascal. He made important contributions in a range of subjects, from Probability Theory to Fluid Mechanics. He also devised possibly the world's first calculator for his father, to ease the drudgery of arithmetic in his tax office.

Towards the end of his life Pascal's world views shifted markedly as his Christian faith grew, resulting in a book entitled *Pensées* (*Thoughts on Religion and some other subjects*), an influential apologia, published posthumously.[3] In it he delineated two kinds of mind. On the one hand, there is what he called '*l'esprit de géométrie*', the mind of the geometer, which is analytical, working precisely and methodically according to abstract principles. (These principles are not immediately evident, but, once considered, reasoning becomes generally straightforward.) On the other hand, there is '*l'esprit de finesse*', which is usually translated as 'the intuitive mind'. It is the subtle, rarefied mind that immediately sees how such principles apply without doing any processing, perhaps without having even reflected on the principles beforehand.

Pascal's direction of thought was in marked contrast to what was happening across much of Europe at the time. The seventeenth century is usually characterised as the 'Age of Reason', in which there was a widespread challenge to the traditional dominance of religious institutions. It was a period when natural philosophy steadily gave way to more rigorous experimental method and externally verifiable observation, to *empiricism*, as promoted by Francis Bacon. This empirical approach, much lauded, would eventually help establish the roots of modern computing, and it is not surprising that pioneering computing developments arose in Europe and North

America. The rationalism promoted by these intellectual movements tended to dismiss explanations that made reference to the divine and transcendent. Instead it leaned naturally towards materialism. But in rejecting the authority of religious institutions with regard to the natural world were they throwing out the baby with the bathwater?

Let us return to numbers, for they are fundamental to the story of computing. Allow me to introduce the branch of mathematics called, unsurprisingly, Number Theory. It is often cited by its proponents as 'the queen of mathematics', apparently after a quote by Carl Friedrich Gauss, one of the giants in the field. As a researcher, he delved into all kinds of numbers – whole numbers, rational numbers, irrational numbers, transcendental numbers and various extensions. He liked to decompose them into prime factors, look at how they are distributed in series, and so on. To formally embody the principles he had discovered, he produced *theorems*, general statements about the properties of numbers. Any such theorem depends on *proof*, which comprises logical sequences of statements derived in accordance with inference rules, rooted in a set of axioms.

We can see immediately that such an approach is dependent on language, requires acuity and involves multiple steps, so it naturally lends itself to computation. We should, however, note that Gauss also had a strong sense of aesthetics – it wasn't enough for him to prove a result in any fashion; he felt a strong need to refine how a proof was demonstrated, so that it became *elegant*.

Aesthetics are much cherished by mathematicians; this sense of beauty, which permeates the arts and sciences, is essential to the human experience. This awareness of the aesthetic dimension would have resonated in the place we now know as India, the birthplace of Buddhism, a land blessed by a long history of both religious and mathematical insight. The subcontinent of South Asia is notable for the earliest known evidence of the number zero and nowadays accounts for a substantial proportion of employees in Silicon Valley start-ups.[4] But rather than delving back 2,500 years or becoming preoccupied with present-day developments, we can gain some sense of enduring Indian cultural practices from a time about a hundred years ago, when England was host to an important phase in the development of number theory during the First World War.

It centred around a mathematical prodigy from South India by the name of Srinivasa Ramanujan. He was thoroughly absorbed in the minutiae of mathematics. He would work through vast quantities of examples to get the feel for them, as a means of discovering general properties. Recording numerous results in notebooks, including solutions to hitherto unsolved problems, he eventually had the courage to write to G.H. Hardy FRS at Trinity College, Cambridge. Hardy was one of the foremost mathematicians of his day and insisted on the application of rigorous analytical methods; but whilst he valued discipline, he also recognised creative genius. Upon seeing some samples of Ramanujan's work he found them so remarkable that he did everything he could to bring him across the seas to Cambridge. In 1914 he eventually succeeded, becoming his supervisor at Trinity and forging a bond that would lead to much pioneering research.

To illustrate Ramanujan's facility, we cite a famous episode in which Hardy was visiting Ramanujan whilst he was recovering from some mysterious illness in a nursing home. [Don't worry if you can't follow the sums.] In his greeting, Hardy casually reported the number of his taxi, 1729, as 'boring', to which Ramanujan immediately responded, 'No. It's a very interesting number; it is the smallest number expressible as the sum of two cubes in two different ways: $1729 = 1^3 + 12^3 = 9^3 + 10^3$.' As it stands, it's a fun piece of trivia, but he's actually intimating something more significant, which was only spotted recently when Ken Ono, another number theorist, came across this same example in Ramanujan's later work relating to Fermat's Last Theorem. That celebrated theorem states that for all integers *n*, where n is at least 3, there is no solution for integer values x, y and z to the equation $x^n + y^n = z^n$. If we omit the 'taxi-cab number' on the left hand side of Ramanujan's two equations above, we have a 'near miss' of a counterexample to the theorem; putting $x = 9$, $y = 10$ and $n = 3$, the theorem tells us that there is no whole number z such that its cube, z^3, can equal $9^3 + 10^3$. Yet if we put $z = 12$, we see $1^3 + 12^3$ is just 1 away.[5]

Cambridge life was completely alien to Ramanujan, especially in matters of religion: Hardy was an atheist whereas Ramanujan was a devout Vaishnava Brahmin. His spiritual practice and mathematical exploits went hand in hand; the extraordinary insight he demonstrated arose through a state of deep absorption. He developed a process that led to his mind becoming highly focused and coherent, resulting in his wonderfully expressive and prolific output. Often a vision would arise in his mind's eye, sometimes during his sleep, of equations written out before him. He would then rush to write them down. Attributing them to a divinity, Namagiri (more commonly known as Lakshmi), he remarked that what he received was but a small portion of divine knowledge, of what God could manifest. He had absolute confidence in their correctness, and was not motivated to meticulously prove them.

Ramanujan was thus especially gifted in intuitive

insight. Hardy insisted, however, that in order to advance his career, he had to undertake the business of proof. This Ramanujan found hard to do, at least initially. It was strict guidance, but Hardy was personally very sympathetic to Ramanujan's approach and they shared certain sublime insights. For Hardy was a purist. He saw mathematics as an activity to *do* creatively, with the aim of producing beautiful results and gaining a sense of their profound significance.

So what did numbers mean to Ramanujan? Let's turn to an Indian source, Shiyali Ramamrita Ranganathan, a mathematician and librarian who gathered eye witness accounts from friends describing Ramanujan's spirituality – or, at least, some of its aspects.[6] The recollections of personality may be honey-coated, but the philosophical and spiritual discussions are likely to be authentic. They are significant because they indicate that a human's innate capacity for brilliance goes well beyond the confines of rationality, confines that appear well understood by exponents of ancient traditions.

Thus we learn from Ranganathan about Ramanujan's strict adherence to the rules for a Brahmin, his devotions deep inside the temple, and his extensive knowledge rooted in Hindu scriptures, particularly the Vedas. To one friend, R. Srinivasan, he declared with conviction, 'Sir, an equation has no meaning for me unless it expresses a thought of

God.' Another friend, Prasanta Mahalanobis, recalled him speaking of 'zero' as the symbol of the Absolute (*Nirguṇa Brahman*), that is, the highest Universal Principle to which no qualities can be attributed; it cannot be defined or described by words, lying completely beyond the reach of the human mind. He looked on 'infinity' as the inexhaustible totality of all possibilities capable of becoming manifest in reality. According to Ramanujan, the product of infinity and zero would supply the whole set of finite numbers, whereby each number that emerged would reflect a particular act of creation; it was as though these acts create numerical signatures. These statements were expressed with such enthusiasm that Mahalanobis reflected, '... Sometimes I felt he would have been better pleased to have succeeded in establishing his philosophical theories than in supplying rigorous proofs of his mathematical conjectures.'

Ranganathan follows up the recollections of Ramanujan's various friends and acquaintances with an analysis based on Indian thinking. He writes that the apprehension of knowledge and its furtherance can be achieved with the help of the primary senses and the intellect, and that these two are generally inseparable.

> We shall use the term 'Intellect' to denote the two taken together. Apprehension of knowledge can also be achieved without the mediation of

> the intellect. The mediating agency in this case, we shall denote by the term 'Intuition'. According to Indian tradition, knowledge through intuition is *thing*-dependent and not *doer*-dependent [my italics] ... Intellection can never lead to Total Apprehension. It will always be partial. Even in the case of the best intellectuals, it can at best make only a very close approximation to Total Apprehension, but cannot reach it. In the case of a full-blown intuitionist, intuition will give Total Apprehension. Intuition is Trans-Intellectual.[7]

The immediacy of the thing-dependent view implies that human intuition has a receptivity beyond the physical body, particularly beyond the brain. Echoing the distinction between *l'esprit de finesse* and *l'esprit de géométrie*, Ranganathan maintains that an intuitionist 'sees' instantaneously and does not approximate through the intellectual processes of induction, deduction and proof, which take time. Such seeing has a quality of exceptional purity: hence the knowledge obtained through intuition is totally trustworthy. But at any moment it can fade and there follows a switch to the intellect, at which point 'the intellect will have to test and verify such a piece of knowledge in its own laborious way'. Whereas the intellect approaches intuition as a limiting point, intuition itself has no limiting point, it is an open set. The difference between the two can be masked to some extent through training – for speed in intellectual work can be increased by incessant practice and undivided attention and concentration. However, intellectual thought is physically limited, whereas intuition, he argued, is not.

This discussion is important in assessing the significance of humans and machines. Whilst not specifically Buddhist, the exposition of the mind-beyond-intellect is compatible with Buddhist perspectives and such views would have been well-known at the time of the Buddha. They provide significant background and foundations for the ethical discussion that I will set out later in this book.

Two kinds of mathematician

As to mental processes at work in mathematics, Ranganathan develops his theme with an illuminating section on the process of proof.

> The proof and the verification is the work for a technician in mathematics. It is necessary work, no doubt, and persons should be trained for this technician's work. ... [But] It would have been bad economy, as Hardy said, to have tamed and trained Ramanujan in that way and made a technician of him. Intuition characterised Ramanujan not only as mathematician but also a Man. This was felt by his friends when he was giving religious,

philosophical, or any other non-mathematical expositions to small intimate groups.[8]

These sentiments about technicians are echoed today by Kevin Buzzard, a pure mathematician. Acknowledging that the process of human proof has become increasingly intricate and so might not be water-tight, he encourages his students to use machines to formalise theorems and assist in their proofs. He has remarked, perhaps jokingly and seriously at the same time: 'Computer scientists fix bugs, while we ignore them.'[9] He recognises that machines can generally be relied upon to be consistent, good at checks and applying rules in a valid way, whereas humans are fallible and prone to making mistakes. Being technically flawless is not so important to pure mathematicians as making a significant discovery.

Notice how the topic of contemporary computing has started to creep in! Besides providing insights into the sublime nature of mathematical discovery, what connection might Ramanujan have with computing today? Ramanujan wasn't a computer scientist, but his work continues to have relevance. For example, his *π formula* has inspired infinite series that enable the value of π to be computed accurate to trillions of decimal places. We won't display the formula here, however, because it was rated as the *ugliest* out of sixty that were evaluated in a neurological study![10] Thus we can consider it *utilitarian.*

Furthermore, Ramanujan seemed able to generate results that today can only be explained with reference to more recent computational methods:

> The formulas that Ramanujan had put in his so-called last [lost] notebooks could not have resulted from pure computations because the methods to do such computations were worked out only in the late 1970s and 1980s, many years after his death. He must have had deep insights. It's puzzling how he came to these findings.[11]

Most accounts of Ramanujan's brilliance express puzzlement at how he could derive so many extraordinary results. It is hard to explain from a discipline rooted in an empirical and material point of view, especially if it comes at the expense of a sense of the divine or supramundane. Such a discipline has seen systems of logic developed with positivistic approaches until many philosophers seemingly had no room left for any sense of transcendence, taking their cue from Wittgenstein's declaration, 'Whereof one cannot speak, thereof one should remain silent' (even if, for Wittgenstein himself, that was not the final word).

With the internal and subjective unaddressed, Ramanujan's insights are bound to appear unfathomable, but Indian spiritual traditions have long made it their goal to explore these aspects – *experientially.*

Such internal vision is of paramount importance to spiritual and religious paths, so let us now bring Buddhism into the discussion, with particular reference to the discipline of ethics.

2

Buddhist Ethics

Buddhist transmission

THE BUDDHA ORIGINALLY gave his teachings in person, tailored to his audience, which was comprised of people from all castes of Indian society. Even though he was well-versed in Sanskrit, he preferred to use local dialects. A formal language, let alone one with precise linguistic rules, was not considered important to the practice or to the nature of the Buddha's realisation. After the Buddha's passing, the transmission of his teachings continued orally, but as disagreements over interpretation grew, it was then that a written canon was introduced some hundreds of years later.

Referred to as the *Tipiṭaka*, a Pali term meaning 'three baskets', it comprises *vinaya* (rules of monastic discipline), *suttas* (sermons), and *abhidhamma* (higher teachings).[12] As a kind of condensation, like any record, it loses something of the actual immediacy of the event, but it is a generally reliable reference that still inspires and guides practice. The Pali canon remains the primary source in Sri Lanka and South-East Asia today.

So what is actually recorded? The sublime quality of a vision is often inexpressible, but what it means and its realization can be made accessible. What is articulated, therefore, is a method or methods which may help one to attain such vision. In the first sermon following his Enlightenment, the Buddha declared: 'Vision and knowledge arose in me' about the fundamental realities of our existence – what he termed the 'Four Noble Truths'. These truths are to be realised in sequence: *dukkha* (suffering or unsatisfactoriness); the origin of *dukkha*; the cessation of *dukkha*; and the path leading to deliverance from *dukkha* through the attainment of complete peace and freedom of mind.

These were direct insights, not intellectualised philosophies. Striving to realise this deliverance is the Buddhist goal of life and it must ultimately be in these terms that we consider the subject. The Buddha spells out what deliverance means in practice through the Eightfold Noble Path, which, to paraphrase, means having the right view, creating the right intentions, practising *sīla* (moral virtue) and developing a skilful *samādhi* (meditative concentration). From the numerous encounters recorded, it is evident that the Buddha taught in a pragmatic manner, in a variety of ways according to the listeners' dispositions.

Intention and agency

According to Buddhism those abilities that Ramanujan demonstrated were intentional – he wished for them and directed his mind and faculties towards them. Pursuing a spiritual path requires an ongoing conscious intention; it doesn't just happen by fate, chance or nature, but its efficacy can only be suggested through reasoning based on practical realities.

Meaningful choice is fundamentally a moral decision whereby the quality of intention leads either to happy or unhappy outcomes, subjectively experienced, forming the basis of well-being. The Buddha referred to such intentional actions as *karma*, and observed that they have profound effects for good and ill.[13] This is expressed concisely in the famous opening verses of the *Dhammapada*, a treasury containing hundreds of his sayings:

> All mental states have mind as their forerunner; mind is their chief, and they are mind-made. If one speaks or acts with a defiled mind, then suffering follows one even as the wheel follows the hoof of the draught ox.
>
> All mental states have mind as their forerunner; mind is their chief, and they are mind-made. If

> one speaks or acts with a pure mind, then happiness follows even as one's shadow never leaves.[14]

That being the case, we need to distinguish between pure and impure mind, right and wrong:

> What is good, what is bad? What is right, what is wrong? What ought I to do or not to do? What, when I have done it, will be for a long time my sorrow ... or my happiness?[15]

This lies at the heart of Buddhist ethics.[16] Buddhist teachings indicate that 'happiness' and 'sorrow' are expressions of reward and retribution. Carrying out morally good or virtuous *karma* leads to the accumulation of merit, a kind of fuel for subsequent happy fruits. That payoff is a natural motivation, a necessary starting point, though the Buddha's path aims beyond.

Each person has individual responsibility for their *karma*. No-one else can change it for us. Whoever we are, whatever our state and the prevailing conditions, our actions are volitional. As such we are heirs to our own *karma*.

> I am the owner of my actions, heir to my actions, born of my actions, related through my actions, and have my actions as my arbitrator. Whatever I do, for good or for evil, to that will I fall heir.[17]

These are universal principles. They apply to any

actions – in body, speech and mind – in any context, physical or psychological.

Whilst Ramanujan was not a Buddhist, he exemplified certain qualities that serve as useful illustrations. He was self-reliant and exceedingly strong-willed, making huge, sustained and conscious effort with a pure heart, so his karmic results were very pronounced. Being such a highly focused driving force led naturally to the mathematical results, but they could only arise through a fundamental quality of human beings: *agency*.

In the *Attakārī Sutta* (The Self-Doer), the Buddha expressed such agency as a doer (oneself or other) having six characteristics: initiation, exertion, making effort, steadfastness, persistence and endeavouring.[18] Applied to physical exercise, becoming fit and strong requires that one is able to take the initiative and apply physical effort, not just once, but over an extended period of time. There isn't anyone else who can do this for us.

Such agency is necessary when gradually progressing along a spiritual path. With right practice it gives rise to various positive outcomes 'visible in the here and now', resulting directly from renunciation and virtuous conduct. The more advanced stages lead to great mental clarity and, beyond that, to higher knowledge (*abhiññā*) accompanied by rarefied capacities such as the 'divine ear' and 'encompassing the minds of others'.[19] We observe that Ramanujan could develop extraordinary abilities by maintaining his Brahminical practices with exacting diligence, particularly in terms of his moral code of conduct. Despite his ardent desire to further his mathematics he wouldn't cross the seas to England until he was convinced that he had special divine dispensation. And, once in England, he maintained his vegetarianism very strictly, in the smallest detail, declining the privileges of college dining halls. Ramanujan was thus assiduously practising *sīla*, which was a necessary foundation for his success.

Buddhist notions of *sīla* may be fundamentally expressed according to the principles of *vāritta* (avoidance) and *cāritta* (positive performance), as in the exhortation in the *Dhammapada*:

> Cease to do evil. Cultivate good. Purify the mind.

In traditionally Buddhist countries, it is customary for lay people to observe a code of conduct or rules of training called 'the Five Precepts'. These are usually formulated as *vāritta*:

1. Refraining from taking life.
2. Refraining from taking that which is not given.
3. Refraining from sexual immorality.
4. Refraining from false speech.
5. Refraining from intoxicants that lead to heedlessness.

It might at first seem counterintuitive to restrict how one behaves as a means to fulfilment, but diligently observing these rules is enabling. It becomes more obvious when considering the *cāritta* counterpart, which is to cultivate compassion, generosity, contentment, honesty and heedfulness – qualities widely regarded as the characteristics of a model member of society. Indeed, the first four precepts have a direct correspondence with the declaration of a Global Ethic affirming four basic human rights.[20] (A link with the Fifth Precept is absent, which is unfortunate as breaking this precept makes one vulnerable to breaking any of the others.)

The quality of choice involved here is a world apart from merely having numerous menu options – so-called 'consumer choice'. For such possessions do not really bring about well-being in society.[21] Knowing this, monastic life is organised according to more stringent rules with a radically reduced number of options. This allows any choice to become more real, to be exercised with heightened awareness and greater restraint. Less is more – as in more peace of mind.

Meditation and mindfulness

The search for the increasingly elusive quality of inner peace has prompted growing interest in meditation and mindfulness. Meditation practice has two stages: the development of calm and clarity and, once sustained, its continuation alongside the cultivation of insight. Mindfulness is a key tool, whereby one rests one's attention internally on an object, such as the breath, the abdomen, or the centre of body. The use of the imagination – visualising something simple and natural like the full moon, for example – can also aid the process of gaining clarity and brightness. In its bare form, mindfulness is the cultivation of awareness, moment to moment; when practised skilfully it brings deep satisfaction, unlike the search for entertainment or distraction, which does not lead to lasting fulfilment.

Repetitive tasks should not be rejected as 'boring'. One of my former meditation teachers used to tell a story about his first job, where he was working on a factory assembly line. His duty was to take a part from one conveyor belt and join it to a part from another conveyor belt. Initially he found it tedious, but after a while he became absorbed, so much so that he didn't want to break for lunch. To bring the mind to a standstill, to peace, helps us to appreciate doing simple things, especially with the whole body. In fact, working with such 'drudgery' is basic to fashioning the mind, rather like metalwork, which requires continual application through not-so-beautiful states. We can deepen our learning and cultivate our mind by doing the same task over and over. This helps to explain how Ramanujan's frequent working with numerical examples helped him to originate so much.

Thanks to a surge in popularity in recent decades, many people have some familiarity with mindfulness practice; it has matured to the point of becoming a standard clinical treatment recommended by the NHS. But what the NHS doesn't really emphasise is that mindfulness is most effective when it is imbued with an ethical perspective. Without such a moral viewpoint, it becomes more a matter of mundane operational efficiency.

In Buddhism, mindfulness and moral agency combine with a keen sensitivity to steer us away from transgression. There are two kinds: a sensitivity to *hiri* (internal moral shame), where contemplating an immoral deed brings a sense of discomfort that rests on one's conscience; whilst *ottappa* (moral dread) is sensitivity to the external effects, such as loss of face. Thoughts of breaking the Precepts give rise to both. They are thus described as 'guardians of the world'.[22] Both are central to what it means to be a human being; and both require the cultivation of awareness.

Guarding against moral transgressions requires another quality, a certain kind of mindfulness, *heedfulness*, the goal of the Fifth Precept, the training to refrain from intoxicants.[23] So important is this quality that the Buddha's last recorded words in the Pali canon are: 'All conditioned phenomena are subject to decay: strive on with heedfulness.'

Without the ethical dimension, the path towards well-being dries up very quickly. We need to keep this in mind as we explore how we use computing in society.

3

Computers and Intelligence

The development of computing

WHAT IS A computer? A general definition may run along the following lines:

> A *computer* is a mechanical device that receives *input* and uses this as *data* on which to carry out logical processing according to a set of instructions specified in a *program*. It may store its workings in memory, generate some output and perform other actions.

The mechanical device is commonly called *hardware*, and the program *software*. Nowadays most computers are electronic and the storage and processing of data is numerical, where quantities are represented as digits, usually in binary form, i.e. as sequences of 0s and 1s. Hence we use the term *digital computer*.

With numbers lying at the heart of computing and

computers, the early devices, as we have seen with Pascal's calculator, were built to solve specific kinds of mathematical problems. In such devices, where 'programming' consisted of rotating dials, turning knobs and cranking handles, everything was integral, in a single unit. But then a breakthrough was made in the early nineteenth century when the first general-purpose computer, the Analytical Engine, was conceived by Charles Babbage.[24] He made a clear separation between the computational hardware and the software, whose instructions were to be written on punched cards.

To solve a given problem, Babbage would work out a sequence of instructions to determine its solution – what we now refer to as an *algorithm.* However, being immersed in the systems architecture required to support low-level logical operations of the engine, he had limited time to disseminate the programming possibilities. It was his mathematical collaborator, Ada the Countess of Lovelace, who really made known and highlighted the distinct field of software development in her English translation of a report about the machine.[25] There she wrote extended notes to describe its capabilities more fully, including a step-by-step guide to how an algorithm can generate Bernoulli numbers (number sequences which are used in many fields of mathematics, including Fermat's Last Theorem).

The Analytical Engine was never built, but what would such machines have been capable of? In her notes, Lovelace reflected on the implications, seeing the potential of the engine to compute symbols, not just numbers, and thus yielding applications in the arts:

> Supposing, for instance, that the fundamental relations of pitched sounds in the science of harmony and of musical composition were susceptible of such expression and adaptations, the engine might compose elaborate and scientific pieces of music of any degree of complexity or extent.[26]

It was not until about a hundred years later that the foundations of modern computing were reprised and developed further, epitomised in the work of Alan Turing, one of the pioneers who presented the formal foundations of computability. In a seminal paper he conceived an abstract computer, now referred to as a *Turing Machine*, which pared down computation to the lowest level in terms of inputs, outputs, processing and storage.[27] He designed it, mathematically speaking, with the greatest expressivity; anything a modern digital computer can do can be computed, in theory, on a Turing Machine.

A few decades later the pivotal roles of Babbage and Lovelace were reflected in the creation of eponymous but very distinct languages: *Babbage* is an assembly language for particular GEC hardware whilst *Ada* is a general-purpose high-level language. The latter has been used in particular to implement artificial intelligence (AI).

Artificial Intelligence?

Whilst the association sounds flattering, Lovelace herself might have been bemused. Having had the foresight to see how a machine like the Analytical Engine might evolve, she also saw its limitations and cautioned against overstating its significance:

> It is desirable to guard against the possibility of exaggerated ideas that might arise as to the power of the Analytical Engine ... The Analytical Engine has no pretensions whatever to *originate* anything. It can do whatever we *know how to order it* to perform.[28]

The key term is 'originate'. What does she mean by it? Lovelace continues:

> It can *follow* analysis; but it has no power of *anticipating* any analytical relations or truths. Its province is to assist us to making *available* what we are already acquainted with.

Without giving an explicit definition, Lovelace implies some of its qualities through negation: one who has originality has the ability to reach truthful conclusions in advance of normal mechanical workings, which I liken to an experienced medical doctor reaching the correct diagnosis after asking just a few choice questions. Originality is not the same as imitation or mimicry, even if these lead to new and unpredictable kinds of outputs. In Pascal's terminology, these machines are consummate in *l'esprit de géométrie* but completely lack *l'esprit de finesse*.

In personal correspondence, Lovelace emphasised the importance of imagination in the process of origination:

> Imagination is the *Discovering* Faculty, pre-eminently ... It is that which feels & discovers what *is*, the REAL which we see not, which exists not for our *senses* ... Mathematical science shows what *is*. It is the language of unseen relations between things ... Imagination too shows what is ... Hence she is or should be especially cultivated by the truly Scientific, those who wish to enter into the worlds around us![29]

It is about being intuitive, spontaneous, and able to synthesise. It is *not* pre-meditated. Like Ramanujan, Lovelace possessed intuitive perception together with a remarkable faculty of concentration. She was able to bring together disparate insights to envisage novel applications of mathematical results.

Turing went on to consider the broad implications

in terms of mind, expressing his results in an influential paper.[30] In it he disagreed with Lovelace as to the significance of discovery, quoting a biblical text (Ecclesiastes 1:9): 'There is nothing new under the sun.' He suggested that all thoughts were simply the result of growth from natural processes or training, all of which could be well-defined, thereby positing *machine learning*. Nevertheless he admitted: 'I do not expect this reply to silence my critic. He will say that [they] ... are due to some creative mental act.'

Turing heralded the arrival of the subject of machine intelligence, with the phrase 'artificial intelligence' being coined a few years later.[31] It came with a new kind of AI ideology proposing a range of bold hypotheses, including:

- A machine is capable of imitating the effects of human activities.
- A machine is capable of thinking in the same way as a human mind, possibly in other ways.

The first is known as a *weak AI* hypothesis, the second a *strong AI* hypothesis. Their advocates point to the ever-increasing computational capacity available in machines as well as their performances, which have already surpassed humans in abstract strategic challenges such as the sophisticated board games of chess and Go. Yet, ever since Turing's own formulation of Gödel's incompleteness theorems, there have been philosophical arguments which highlight certain limitations in any formal system's capacity to prove what is true, limitations to which humans are not subject. So the 'strong AI' hypothesis would appear to be false, at least for the given notion of 'machine'. It is the subject of much discussion. One of the most notable exponents of the view of non-computability of thought is the mathematician and physicist, Sir Roger Penrose. He amply illustrates this himself through strikingly original and ingenious demonstrations, such as his non-repeating tessellations.[32]

Buddhist tradition would also assert that humans are capable of proceeding along non-algorithmic pathways, as witnessed in the sublime and vivid meditation experiences which arise spontaneously and defy description. Real intelligence lies in seeing and knowing this experience subjectively, knowing its significance with respect to the conditioned and unconditioned. This cannot be adequately conveyed through philosophical argument, but we can at least point beyond the merely rational.

What is intelligence?

As human beings we have the capacity to originate ideas and to understand their significance, which is what properly defines us as intelligent. In the absence of any denotational proof, we can nevertheless suggest its validity with reference to *savants*, who are often characterised as human supercomputers diagnosed with a kind of autism. Being unable to articulate the processes by which they calculate, they are commonly – and lazily – regarded as unaware 'freaks of nature' and hence likened to computing machines. One savant, Daniel Tammet, says this is a great mistake: 'Very often the analogy has been that a savant is like a computer, but what I do is about as far from what a computer does as you can imagine.' Tammet has described his relationship with numbers in terms very similar to those ascribed to Ramanujan:

> I have a relationship with numbers that is similar to the relationship that most people have with language. When people think of words, they don't think of them as separate items, atomised in their head, they understand them intuitively and subconsciously as belonging to an interconnected web of other words.[33]

Tammet distinguishes between his working with numbers, which he regards as holistic, and the discrete processing executed by computing machines. He echoes the sentiments expressed by Kevin Buzzard in his distinction between the nature of the research carried out by pure mathematicians and that of verifying proofs.

Let us return to the question, intimated above

for AI: can a computer think? It depends on the definition, but it is generally accepted that thinking requires consciousness. The word 'consciousness' is derived from Latin, *cum* ('with') plus *scire* ('to know'), which means knowing in relation to something. It comprises internal and external awareness and its various subtleties can lead to many kinds of response.

From a Buddhist perspective, this a subjective quality that can be ascribed to all sentient beings - including humans, celestial beings, ghosts, animals and beings in realms of deprivation. In Buddhist cosmology these beings are usually described as having a stream of consciousness subject to *Samsara*, the endless round of rebirth. According to the Buddha's teaching we quoted from the Dhammapada, that consciousness has a moral basis, conditioned by actions in body, speech and mind; if the actions are bright and virtuous the forms and states they condition are happy, whereas if they are dull and impure the results are woeful. Here a characteristic response might be: conscious of our own predicament, we express loving kindness and compassion to them with the wish, 'May all beings be well and happy.'

The Buddha taught that with the right practice and the right application, we can see clearly what's going on and go beyond Samsara. He used a special term, the 'Dhamma eye', for a transcendent faculty we may develop, even enabling one to observe the observer. It is possessed by all those who have attained Enlightenment. Such awareness cannot be 'built into' a machine; it doesn't become sentient through emulation in embedded software, though conceivably some consciousness of a living being might dwell there. Thinking also requires originality, else it becomes mere cogitation. Yet humans can be fooled into thinking that artificial semblances are real and sentient. They can also be reduced to behaving like machines, performing the same routines without any awareness.

The tech industry uses many terms associated with intelligence; we hear so much about 'big data' as the key to a better understanding of the world and to 'smart living' that it is becoming like a mantra. But are we looking down the wrong end of the telescope? Allow me to offer an alternative view of intelligence, based on the characteristics of a Buddha expounded in the daily chant, *iti pi so* (literally, '*He is indeed*').[34] Here the Buddha is declared an *arahat,* one who has attained *nibbāna* (final release from Samsara), and is furthermore 'supremely self-Enlightened'; he is consummate in insight into the nature of supramundane reality, and he truly knows the phenomenal world, together with the workings of *karma.* The suttas also describe him possessing *paññā,* the intuitive wisdom and discernment that aids progress along the path. The condensation of such wisdom might be regarded as *knowledge*, supported intellectually by information and data.

Across the globe, society has moved towards the end of this list, tending to dwell on the material with an ever-increasing focus on externalised measurement and assessment. As a consequence, ethical responsibility has been shifted from the individual and personal toward the collective and impersonal. In such an environment, outward conformity to society norms and organisational regulation plays a major role, with greater emphasis on legalistic notions of 'individual choice' and 'rights'; transgression has a tendency to become someone else's 'fault' because of 'infringing on these rights.'

In contrast, according to Buddhist teachings, those who are 'intelligent' (normally rendered in translation as 'the wise') are able to discern the *ethical value* of someone's individual actions in terms of the karmic results: do they increase or decrease *dukkha,* that existential dis-ease associated with moral degeneration and decline, rooted in ignorance? Hence, the teachings advise, 'Do not do something that the wise would later reprove.' And, again in the *iti pi so*, the Dhamma preached by the Buddha is 'to be realised individually by the wise'. This type of thinking is not externally measurable and so lies beyond the scope of utility and machines.

What roles for AI?

The foregoing evaluation from an ethical standpoint reveals some of the limitations of algorithms and machines, but in so doing clarifies their role. By recognising their proper place we might be generally wiser when we ask the question: What are the *right* roles for artificial intelligence?

Common perceptions currently run as follows. On the one hand, there is great excitement about the potential to improve the efficiency of complex operations, to ease the drudgery of work, to provide new healthcare benefits and even to address poverty in its various forms. Problems that were previously regarded as computationally intractable now appear within reach with the prospect of quantum computing. On the other hand, there is no shortage of apocalyptic scenarios about systems going berserk or being manipulated by unscrupulous parties if we get it wrong – and many such outcomes are becoming feasible.

In short, most of the potential benefits are material, but the untethered expansion of services risks abuse. We may well ask: Why the headlong rush when the Buddha and many of his disciples needed none of this technology to attain Enlightenment? In fact, his monastic followers were required to possess a mere eight articles (bowl, robes, and other requisites).

Devices to assist or extend human capacity have

long existed; walking sticks, glasses, hearing aids and so on. However, even physical aids can be counter-productive: if a person recovering from injury relies too much on a Zimmer frame, for example, they might not build up sufficient strength to walk independently. For mental aids, analogously, dependence can impair innate ability; always turning to electronic calculators for one's sums can lead to helplessness in everyday situations – as we shall see.

Many spiritual traditions share this emphasis on treating patients as a whole rather than as a set of discrete components or symptoms. They argue that this has a far more sustainable long-term impact, but investment is often lacking in the face of treatments that offer very narrowly defined, but measurable, benefits.

In assessing technology, we need to consider especially the impact on our ability to make genuine and significant choices, choices that if taken correctly lead us to reflect, 'I'm really glad I did that.' At home and at work, we should be aware of the various activities going on. We should be guarding the sense doors (inputs through eyes, ears, nose, mouth, body and mind), noting their effects. In the world of computer hardware security, it is sometimes said that a safe machine is one that is disconnected from any network and which disregards all inputs. If and when connected, it is constantly monitoring electronic traffic at various levels, moderating the flow of data, taking samples to check that it doesn't contain malign patterns, and so on. Perhaps a diligent human being should be doing something similar if they don't wish to be overrun with intrusive and potentially harmful influences? (Or at least regularly take time offline or go on a digital 'retreat'.[35])

Living with technology implies a major mental overhead and we should ask ourselves: Is it worth it? What is really valuable and how might we nurture this in the best way? The marketing of AI would suggest that humans can be 'enhanced' by intelligent algorithms; but if we accept that humans are creative in ways that machines can never be, then who or what is really benefitting? This becomes particularly pertinent with biological-machine interfaces, a research area which has generated a lot of interest and which is receiving increasing investment. Software is already making use of human input: search engines learn from our queries. By the same token, software embedded in the human body, especially if connected with the brain, can draw on human capacity. This gives rise to the possibility that machines become parasites, with our bodies 'network-enabled', a node in the 'Internet of Things'. Who is in control then?

We should challenge our use of technology with questions such as: Does it help to deepen and enrich our lives? Does the mind gain internal assurance?

To help us evaluate, especially with respect to our freedom to choose, we can apply each element in the *Attakārī Sutta*, as introduced previously in the discussion on intention and agency. What are the effects of a proposed technology-based solution on: personal autonomy, initiation, making effort, exerting oneself, steadfastness, persistence and endeavouring?

Going through the list, I would suggest that different weightings ought to be applied: the most important being autonomy, for if we have no autonomy we become passive, unable to make choices, and the other qualities become null and void. We may go so far as to say that a technological service may be deemed a success if users find that its adoption enables them to be increasingly able to live *without* it, to become mentally and emotionally stronger and more independent.

In this light let us consider the example of the calculator.

- *Autonomy:* It can broadly help us to carry out more complex sums to fulfil various tasks at home and at the office. However, a reliance on technology can weaken our ability to reason in everyday situations where we don't have access to a calculator. Sometimes we have to make a quick evaluation, with no time to press buttons. Also, in general reasoning we may be dealing with numbers in our heads – as when assessing proportions, dealing with dates, times, and so on.

- *Initiation:* We switch on the calculator and enter the sum: OK. Someone does that for us: not OK?
- *Effort:* A few taps require almost no effort. The parts of the brain that perform mental arithmetic are barely engaged; over time, like other underused muscles, they will perform less well.
- *Exertion and steadfastness:* mental arithmetic requires concentration. A complex calculation needs greater effort. If we are not used to this, then we give up more easily. With a range of electronic gadgets at our disposal, it is easy to become lazy.
- *Persistence:* Allowing calculators to solve complex problems brings rapid results, but also means we can lack the understanding of the underlying methods, so we are at a loss to tackle them without the devices to hand. As Ramanujan showed, persistence with repetitive tasks can increase understanding and lead to novel insights.
- *Endeavouring:* A desire to explore mathematics in all its richness is unlikely to arise if a calculator is used all the time.

Overall, it is a boon to have a calculator for complex calculations, but we should maintain our ability to carry out mental arithmetic for simpler sums. If not, the convenience of using a calculator comes at the expense of our own ability, which needs training. The same observation applies to other gadgets such as satnav. I invite you to analyse it likewise to answer the question: how does the use of satnav affect our capacity to find our way around?

Being cautious about the potential impact, we could introduce a kind of anthropomorphic mindfulness bell, which would ring every time we introduce technologies that replicate natural human activities – such as *social* networking, artificial *intelligence*, *autonomous* systems. We should evaluate them: do they help us to improve, independently of such technology, social networking, intelligence, autonomy, etc.? With that in mind, we can move on from this simple example to apply the same approach to evaluate more intricate use cases. We will explore this topic in more detail when it comes to the design of social networking sites, the subject of chapter 5; but first let us take a closer look at processes, for Buddhism and computing have much to say about them.

4

Modelling Mind and Processes

Phenomena and processes

WE MAY EXAMINE Buddhism and computing on a deeper level by seeing how they model phenomena and processes. Here I would like to introduce some concepts concerning the building blocks of existence (and their evanescence) and how they might be formally represented so as to aid reasoning. Intimating such novel connections makes this chapter somewhat more technical than the others, but much of this is just terminology so it's worth persevering. Once you grasp the logic it should be much more straightforward (we hope!).

The Buddha was primarily teaching about an individual's path to liberation and not about natural science. He made a basic distinction between the *conditioned* and the *unconditioned*, pointing out that without the latter there would be no liberation.[36] Most of the time, however, he was concerned with dealing with the problem at hand, which was entrenched in the conditioned. Accordingly this is where his analysis, diagnosis and treatment are conducted; most of the teachings make reference to this context.

What does 'the conditioned' cover? It covers all phenomena, termed *nāmarūpa*, where *nāma* translates approximately as 'mind' and *rūpa* as 'matter'. Being mutually dependent, they are taken together and hence referred to as 'the psychophysical'. They are also synonymous with the five *khandhas* (literally, 'heaps' or 'bundles'), where *nāma* is presented as four distinct aspects: *vedanā* (feelings), *saññā* (perception), *sankhārā* ('things made or done together', mental formations) and *viññāṇa* (consciousness).[37]

The *khandhas* are to be understood in terms of interconnected processes as experienced by an individual. For example, in the seeing of an object such as a flower (*rūpa)*, a physical impression (*vedanā*) is registered in the eye, which is generally pleasant, unpleasant or neutral, together with consciousness of it (*viññāṇa)*. This threefold process applies to each sense: seeing, hearing, taste, touch, smell and mind objects (in Buddhism there are five physical senses plus a sixth for mind). Usually they are also accompanied by *saññā*, which is a process of measurement and recognition involving size, shape, colour, texture and other attributes.

Saññā draws on further sense data from *vedanā* and interpretation from *sankhārā*, into which it also feeds. In this way *sankhārā* acts as a consumer-producer, with access to many layers of storage, including patterns of behaviour that become ingrained as habitual tendencies. Depending on our intentions, these tendencies can be reinforced actively and passively through actions in body, speech and mind. However they are acted upon, they are ever-changing. This process happens continually and largely defines in conventional terms who we are. This is why it is so important to know how we condition and are in turn conditioned by our environments.

To this process-oriented view the Buddha brought in the ethical dimension, whose principles we introduced previously. Intrinsic to the Eightfold Noble Path, 'right thought' points beyond the *khandhas* to the supramundane reality of the unconditioned, where the distinction between 'right' and 'wrong' thought is based on wisdom – in the selection and cultivation of the path out of suffering (*dukkha*) to *nibbāna*. Focused on this process of liberation, the Buddha taught a path of purification, repeatedly pointing out the perils of the 'clinging *khandhas*', the basis of various kinds of attachment covering material and mental objects. Such attachment leads to frustration and woe, he argued, not to fulfilment and happiness. It is a kind of factory operating around the clock, in which the role of the *sankhārā* is pivotal, storing results of volitional activities and conditioning future formations of *nāmarūpa*. In this factory the subjective-objective are made integral, only hinted at in certain scientific fields such as quantum mechanics where the 'observer effect' (affecting or creating system outcomes) has suggested some interconnection.

Khandhas can be viewed impersonally. From this perspective, computers are *rūpa*, and consciousness of their operations is *viññāṇa,* an aspect of *nāma*, but the *rūpa* does not originate any *nāma*. Immediately we see that machines cannot become conscious by themselves. Yet, the suttas present more startling claims: the Buddha gave meditation instructions for the obtaining of several so-called 'formless realms' where there is *viññāṇa* without *rūpa*, i.e. consciousness beyond the brain.[38]

If we focus on processes in a more tangible way, we can make further observations that contrast computing with what is involved in directing the mind. In terms of hardware, computers generally have one or more central processing units (CPUs) operating at a specified speed, usually optimised for performance balanced against the requirements of energy conservation. The pauses in processes (whether at CPU or higher level) do not generally contribute to the *quality* of the outcome beyond various kinds of internal management such as workflows (enabling other processes to complete), resources (memory allocation and 'garbage collection'), power consumption, maintaining thermal conditions, and so on. In other words, the benefits to pausing don't affect the nature of the computation.

It is entirely different when it comes to the mind, especially during meditation practice, where pausing can fundamentally change the outcome. When the mind starts to relax, this has both physiological and psychological effects. The body becomes more pliant, breathing becomes easier. With less activity in the body, the brain needs less oxygen to process, the thoughts start to ease and the body relaxes further. The reduction of activity (in doing and processing) leads to a settled mind.

When the mind is at a complete standstill, then something else may happen. It may access another level of awareness, with new kinds of perception, fresh insight, and so on. Thus pausing the mind has a 'vertical' quality, going *deeper*. This may change the regions of activation in the brain or even not be registered there. It is in such stillness that more profound realisations may emerge. Some of the words associated with such states are: 'floating', 'clarity', 'brightness', 'illumination', 'connected', and 'unified'. We may say that *stopping* is the sign of success! In more prosaic terms, one may be continually working on a problem for hours and reach a sticking point. It's only by letting go that something 'pops up', and there's a breakthrough. It can happen after meditation, sleep or whilst travelling on the bus, anywhere where habitual rumination ceases.

Much may be made of Buddhist insights being in contradistinction to computing processes, but it is now time to consider a more constructive role for computing, and one that can inform Buddhism positively.

Process algebras

The Buddha taught methods to cultivate the mind, usually in sequence: one step follows another, in order, directing the mind inwards – for it is 'within this fathom-long body that there is the world and the end of the world.'[39] At each step, the mode of behaviour may appear to be repeated. Indeed the canonical texts are full of various kinds of repetition, sometimes making them unwieldy and tedious to study. Formalising these processes as mathematical models can bring clarity and precision: the notation has a much simpler syntax than everyday language and can incorporate basic structuring elements, including repetition of steps, or 'recursion' as it is known. This makes it easier to identify distinctive patterns, thus helping us to sharpen our understanding.

Let us therefore adopt a family of formal languages called *process algebras,* as defined below:

> Process Algebras are mathematically rigorous languages with well defined semantics that permit describing and verifying properties of concurrent communicating systems. They can be seen as models of processes, regarded as agents that act and interact continuously with other similar agents. The agents may be real-world objects (even people), or they may be artefacts, embodied perhaps in computer hardware or software systems.[40]

They have the advantage of being both expressive and quite legible, not crowded with symbols. Their flexibility allows the modelling of human interactions with the environment – our daily activities or even subjective experience.

To illustrate, I'd like to choose a specific process algebra called LOTOS (Language of Temporal Ordering Specification).[41] In LOTOS, a system consists of *processes* whose states change through *observable* (or externally visible) *behaviour* composed of *actions.* Originally designed for communication systems, *actions* are synonyms for *gates* and are thus participants in an *environment* where every action occurs as a *synchronisation* of processes.

Actions may be composed sequentially, separated by the action prefix operator ';', and end with a *behaviour expression* (representing a *state* of a process) in capitals. For example, 'get up'; 'wash'; 'get dressed'; 'have breakfast'; GOING_TO_WORK. Behaviour expressions themselves can be composed sequentially, separated by '>>'.

At each state, unless we've reached deadlock, there is always some action that may be performed. Typically there are a number of options, which are modelled as a composition using the *choice* operator, '[]'. As a very simple example, suppose a person is retiring for the night and considers whether to sleep immediately or to meditate beforehand. This might be represented by the fragment:

```
sleep; RESTED
[]
meditate; sleep; SUPER_RESTED
```

Choices may include *deterministic* processes alongside *non-deterministic* ones, i.e. actions that take place independently of the environment, which could be random or – from the point of view of a human actor – an intentional action, conscious and purposeful. These are prefixed by a special *internal action*, **`i`**, indicating some inner process hidden from the environment that leads to the following action. So, if we regard sleep as an automatic action and meditation as a conscious decision, then the latter could be modelled as:

i; meditate; sleep; SUPER_RESTED

Externally, there appears to be no difference, but internally there is and it comes with effort. This becomes significant when considering the evolution of a process, how events may unfold: in LOTOS actions or gates are regarded as controllers in which internal action steers the course of subsequent actions away from environmental control. On the other hand, many actions happen automatically – for instance, our physical motors continue when walking whilst our consciousness dwells elsewhere.

Formalising Buddhist models in LOTOS

LOTOS lends itself well to modelling Buddhist concepts: defining systems explicitly in terms of *actions* naturally suggests a parallel with *karma* and the *synchronisation* appears capable of modelling interrelatedness. The potential to assist in reasoning about Buddhist teachings may be illustrated with reference to the Twelve Links of Dependent Origination, a key doctrine that expresses how phenomena arise in dependence on other phenomena.[42] The doctrine describes each element in the causal chain, starting with ignorance. Ignorance conditions volitional activity – actions of thought, word and deed – which in turn conditions consciousness. Proceeding through a linked succession we reach birth, which conditions old age and death. This sequence, in summary, expresses the statement: 'This being, that becomes; this ceasing, that ceases.'

If life were completely deterministic then this chain would operate in perpetuity, sustaining the eternal round, but there are two places where it can be broken: one is right at the beginning – by dispelling ignorance through higher knowledge. The other is between feeling and craving, the deep-rooted thirst that underpins greed, hatred and delusion, fuelling the cycle of *dukkha*. It's at this point that mindfulness takes aim, seeking to weaken the usual corrupting tendencies.

Process algebras allow us to formally model these phenomena as sequences of events or states. They may include choices; hence the critical stage we've highlighted might look like:

```
feeling;
(
 craving; LESS_PEACE
[]
 i; non_craving_mindfulness; MORE_PEACE
)
```

The formula is saying that after feeling, if one consciously practises mindfulness without craving then one attains a more peaceful state. However, if this mindfulness is absent, then there is some craving (if it's pleasant, we want more, but if unpleasant we want less).

Process algebras are especially designed for modelling *communicating* and *concurrent* processes, which in Buddhist terms we can think of as phenomena arising and passing in dependence on a multitude of conditions. We have already mentioned that in LOTOS, interactions with the environment (and thus interdependence between agents) occur through synchronisation. Accordingly, the *synchronisation* operator specifies how agents perform together in some environment: acting independently is denoted by ||| (*interleave* operator), whereas a set of actions, a_1, a_2, ... that agents are constrained to perform together is denoted $| \langle a_1, a_2, \ldots \rangle |$. A telephone call might be modelled, JANE | *chat* | JOE.

As a general application, *sankhārā* can be modelled as consumer-producer operating in tandem with a 'channel' of the conditioned environment – for *karma* doesn't operate in a vacuum. In this channel there can be actions that model both the subjective (a consumer receiving sense impressions) and the objective (a producer offering memories and other data to the perceiving process). In particular, we may model humans and online media services as parallel agents where synchronisation happens on actions denoting our use or consumption of those services.

When applying modularity we find multiple synchronisations taking place at the same time – across our senses. In consuming these services, absorbed by the *sankhārā*, our memory stores are augmented and habitual tendencies reinforced. It is generally one-way traffic; we tune in and passively receive and digest the content (including the advertising).

To indicate the potential of this approach more fully, let us zoom in on this process of consumption as we attempt to model part of the *Chachakka Sutta*.[43] This sutta gradually teaches how to deal with dependent origination through the six senses. It is highly repetitive. The extract below describes one of the sextets of the teaching:

> 'The six classes of consciousness should be known.' Thus was it said. In reference to what was it said? Dependent on the eye & forms there arises consciousness at the eye. Dependent on the ear & sounds there arises consciousness at the ear. Dependent on the nose & aromas there arises consciousness at the nose. Dependent on the tongue & flavours there arises consciousness at the tongue. Dependent on the body & tactile sensations there arises consciousness at the body. Dependent on the intellect & ideas there arises consciousness at the intellect. 'The six classes of

> consciousness should be known.' Thus was it said. And in reference to this was it said. This is the third sextet.

It continues in this vein for the next class, concerning contact, followed by feeling and then craving, each section augmenting the previous one with a further statement for each case. Thus, we have for the eye:

> Dependent on the eye & forms there arises consciousness at the eye. The meeting of the three is contact. With contact as a requisite condition there is feeling. With feeling as a requisite condition there is craving.

The Buddha then goes on to reverse the last step, in a process about discernment at the point of feeling as a key to liberation whereby conditions for craving are eliminated (echoing the example above).

In LOTOS each case may be rendered using *behaviour definitions* (starting with the keyword **process**), which are instantiated by *parameters* - rather like a *procedure*, a ubiquitous feature in computing. A partial formalisation that captures the classes of consciousness and a little of the subsequent process might look like this:

```
behaviour
 (
 KNOW_CONSCIOUSNESS [eye, forms, eye-consciousness] >>
 KNOW_CONTACT [eye, forms, eye-consciousness] >>
 KNOW_FEELING [eye, forms, eye-consciousness] >>
 KNOW_CRAVING [eye, forms, eye-consciousness] >>
 KNOW_NOT_SELF [eye, forms, eye-consciousness] >>
RIGHTLY_DISCERN_CONTACT_PLEASURE_NOPLEASURE [eye,
forms, eye-consciousness] >>
 exit_Samsara
 )
 ||| ... |||
 (
 KNOW_CONSCIOUSNESS [intellect, ideas, intellect-consciousness]
>>
 KNOW_CONTACT[intellect, ideas, intellect-consciousness] >>
 ... exit_Samsara
 )
where
process KNOW_ CONSCIOUSNESS [sense, sense_object,
sense_consciousness] :=
 ((sense; sense_object; exit) [] (sense_object; sense; exit))
>> sense_consciousness; exit
endproc
process KNOW_ CONTACT [sense, sense_object, sense_consciousness]
:=
 KNOW_ CONSCIOUSNESS [sense, sense_object, sense_consciousness]
>> contact; exit
endproc
 ...
```

(and so on for knowing feeling, cravings and then discernment).

Whilst the notation may be unfamiliar, a correspondence with the original translation should be discernible. Notice how it highlights common structures. The order of stages is immediately evident and variations are clearly determined by the different senses. It is altogether more concise than a standard representation, even one with liberal use of ellipses. But is this the right model? The use of ||| (interleaving) allows development of practice across all the senses, yet liberation (denoted by the special expression, **exit_Samsara**) is achieved through precisely one of them. Is this what the sutta says?

Special care is needed to take account of subtle variation, for where or how attention is directed has huge implications in practice. It is not unlike playing a piece of music, starting as a beginner and simply trying to play the notes in the right order. With practice the sequence is learnt and then the approach and intonation become deeper, more refined. So whilst some of the repetitive nature to the texts is formulaic (and almost certainly added later, as the result of subsequent editorial work) the unexpurgated transcript should help to establish in listeners a rhythm in practice close to that conveyed in the original sermon.[44] This kind of rhythm is important for retention and reinforcement; if a reading is too concise, it might not sink in.

This suggests that formalisation might be most useful as a study aid to complement meditation practice and critical reflection.

Self and not-self

Process algebras can model psychophysical phenomena at various levels of abstraction in terms of ongoing changes of state. They can then prompt reflections on impermanence that help to dissolve conventional notions of personality. They can in particular describe how our bodies age, right down to the cellular level. Nothing remains the same: all is impermanent and subject to continual processes of change. Typically we associate discomfort with such change – as we get older, we lose our physical looks, the body aches more and there is a general decline in energy levels and vitality. We're not the same as before and no scientific know-how can reverse this; so we see that the body is a source of dis-ease, is impermanent and inherently devoid of permanent self. The Buddhist word for self is *attā*; and its absence, as in this case, is *anattā*, often rendered 'not-self', or 'no fixed self'.

When the Buddha gave a teaching, he was acutely aware of the state of progress of the listener(s) and adjusted his guidance accordingly. In many cases his disciples had seemingly reached a plateau and were stuck, unable to penetrate to a higher level of understanding. The Buddha could usually help, but in some cases the state of mind of his listener needed a subtle change. He perceived that many of these blockages were around attachments to false views of self. On examining phenomenal existence, the Buddha came to the conclusion that all the *khandhas* - form, feelings, perceptions, mental formations and consciousness - are impermanent and thus cannot possess any inherent permanent essence.

This is expressed in the *Chachakka Sutta*. Following the discussions of the link between feeling and craving, the Buddha proceeds to teach that each sense is *anattā*, and likewise for each sense-form, sense-consciousness, feelings and craving. Knowing this aids the dissolution of that link, which the practitioner can then bring about by the practice of rightly discerning feelings as just pleasant, unpleasant or neutral. Note the specific context, which is often signalled by phrases such as 'with reference to'. This is only a statement about *conditioned* phenomena, not the unconditioned; the Buddha never went so far as issuing a general declaration, 'There is no self.'[45]

There are practical reasons why promoting a nihilistic view of self can be a mistake. During her work teaching Buddhism and meditation, my mother found that many practitioners had low self-esteem, typically through failed relationships. To teach 'no self' in sweeping fashion to people in such a vulnerable condition could easily have led to serious psychological problems, so she taught in a way to boost self-confidence. Having a healthy view of self enables one to be centred and, I would argue, is necessary to see clearly the nature of this world and beyond. There is in fact a famous passage where the Buddha exhorts his disciples:

> Therefore fare along with self as island, with self as refuge, and no other, with *dhamma* as island, with *dhamma* as refuge, and no other.[46]

Here '*dhamma*' means 'the norm' or 'reality' rather than some teaching formulae – and it is a grounding found within each person, not outside or elsewhere.

How, then, should we orientate ourselves to notions of 'I' and 'self' in a technology-heavy society, where we are staring at screens and interacting with digital assistants offering to work on our behalf and unburden us? We may usefully start by acknowledging that our society is marked by problems of divided attention and fragmentation. In such a situation we need to guard against practices that lead to mental disintegration, through information overload or atrophy – a particularly strong risk in relation to computers and AI.

If there is no clear sense of identity, or if it is

diffuse, then one can become confused, thinking that it doesn't matter where our attention lies or what constitutes our body or self – as it is all impermanent, just be mindful and let go. With such a view, a sense of autonomy can easily shift, and if we are not careful we will end up abdicating responsibility. Whilst machines may not be conscious, they can certainly model or simulate aspects of the *khandhas*: equipped with sensors, they can process and evaluate inputs, and will respond and interact with their environments with increasing competence.

Now, consider for a moment the practice of mindfulness and clear comprehension. The path of such practice should be coherent and focused. Meditation usually involves working with a single object so that the quality of one-pointedness may be developed, even when the object appears to dissolve. In terms of states of meditative absorption *(jhāna)*, entry to the first *jhāna* starts by directed thought and moves into unification of awareness in the second, and so on to still deeper coherence and finer qualities of discernment. The Middle Way is a most *precise* path that requires looking closely at things and making them clear, especially bringing the right things into view. At each step the path continues along the Middle Way, but the practice becomes steadily more refined.

It is like examining an object under a microscope. We start by bringing the object under the least powerful lens. As we zoom in, we use a higher quality lens with an increased level of magnification for which we need to make finer adjustments to keep the object in view. If we keep the object located at the very centre it will remain in view under our lens, but if we start to deviate, then it can quickly disappear. Certainly, our focus needs to be sharper and more precise to observe the object clearly at that level of magnification.

This recursive approach can be applied to meditation literally and directly by using the centre of our bodies as an object of meditation, finding and working with our centre of gravity. The direction of travel comes from successively zooming in and seeing with increasing clarity and insight – leading onwards and inwards in the exploration of who we are.[47]

5

Designing Sustainable Social Networks

THE BUDDHIST PATH has a lofty goal, yet its pursuit is eminently practical. It comes with innumerable applications in relation to the design of technology and is particularly relevant to a discussion of software services on the Internet. Retaining our focus on ethics, our aim will be to draw out qualitative aspects and their impact on well-being and the spiritual path. To save space we only touch on a few aspects of implementation and roll them into the main discussions on design.

We give primacy to intention and agency, especially the ability to live autonomously, thereby helping to fulfil the six characteristics of the *Attakārī Sutta*. We also try to intimate how this can guide us as we implement such services and utilise AI.

The problem of well-being

During the past two decades we have seen the

Internet increasingly permeate people's lives. We have watched the emergence of so-called *social media* with the likes of Facebook, YouTube, Instagram and WhatsApp each amassing more than a billion 'active users'. In their capacity to build social relationships, they are termed *social networking sites* (SNS for short) and have become – for some – an intrinsic part of life, connecting people and their interests, helping in the formation and sustaining of communities. However, the Internet's evanescent nature has witnessed the majority of such online services, including SNS, spark like fireworks that illuminate the landscape brightly for a very short period before vanishing from view. And even with the most popular services, there is widespread dissatisfaction, weariness, angst and distrust. In a word: *dukkha*!

So what went wrong? Why do many people continue to feel that such services are fundamentally 'broken'? One explanation is that they have over-reached and become unwieldy, having developed far beyond the original context and purpose. Probably a more pertinent explanation is that many initiatives have been increasingly driven by commercial goals. The clarity of the original social vision fades away as it gets turned by degrees into systems for generating profit. In conversation and in online fora the levels of dissatisfaction are high and yet, curiously, it is hard to find mostly unfavourable impressions in the numerous scholarly evaluations of social media. Yes, they say the picture is mixed, but overall there are many positives (and we should be thankful).

There seems to be a striking disparity. Why? Could it have something to do with the nature of the evaluation? Many studies carry out assessments of *well-being*, the term generally used to encapsulate good health in body and mind. What exactly does *well-being* mean in this context? Its sense is usually drawn from the social sciences, where it is typically defined as a subjective view of one's perceived quality of life. We highlight here distinctions noted between brief or fleeting happiness and more long-term contentment:

> Generally speaking, self-ratings of 'happiness' turn out to reflect relatively short-term, situation-dependent expressions of mood, whereas self-ratings of 'life satisfaction' appear to measure longer-term, more stable evaluations.[48]

The distinction between transient and more enduring happiness sounds compatible with Buddhist views; but what lies behind these indications and what facilitates them? According to the literature, a key contributing factor is *social capital*, another term which occurs frequently in academic studies. Despite the fact that there is no standard definition, a certain underlying pattern may be discerned in how systems have been built so far and it carries great significance.

In a broad survey, Alejandro Portes observed that its sense has broadened from pertaining fundamentally to the individual and their family kinships – rooted in the foundational work of nineteenth-century sociologists, particularly Émile Durkheim – to larger-scale social integration.[49] He credits its first systematic treatment to Pierre Bourdieu, who defined it (for an individual) as 'the aggregate of the actual or potential resources which are linked to possession of a durable network of more or less institutionalised relationships of mutual acquaintance or recognition'.[50] Portes illustrates how the research, whilst aspiring to social cohesion, has in fact given rise to many theories that appear equally to allow both positive and negative networks because the definitions of social capital are vague or ambiguous. He observes that the personal concept of 'social capital' based on kinship relationships has gradually evolved to become more impersonal and more generalised.

Indeed, Bourdieu's definition could be satisfied by many kinds of entities, including commercial corporations and federated Internet-based software services, i.e. the systems in which the social capital is being established. Whilst these services are like the close-fitting manifestations or shadows of human activity, they should not be equated with human relationships themselves – if you get to know someone by email, it is evidenced by a record of correspondence, but if you then meet in person you do not need that record or email itself to continue developing the friendship.

The system logs are heavily identified with human activity, and with the interpersonal relationships themselves. But, whilst this readily enables quantification and basic usage figures as garnered for analytics, much of the analysis needs careful interpretation dependent on (often unreliable) self-responses. How then can we reach definite and meaningful conclusions about what is really of value? It is unsurprising that the findings with regard to well-being are very mixed, even in the interpretation of identical data.

A common pattern clearly established with many social media services is that existing bonds are strengthened. But this nourishing of homogeneous networks (people with similar interests and sensibilities) seems to come at the expense of heterogeneous networks (others with differing views). Biases are reinforced and sharp divisions are made, contrasting 'us' and 'them', tending to foster antipathy and antagonism, giving rise to much acrimony. In such situations, where we should be open to criticism, ready to forgive and working for reconciliation, the systems are unable to provide suitable support.

Another common finding is that heavy usage is associated with loneliness; so that whereas the number of loose associations has increased, the number of close friends seems to be reducing. This is corroborated in ethnographic work, which gives a more vivid picture of individual motivations. In his *Material World* blog, Daniel Miller has highlighted the dynamic impetus it gives to social connection, marketing and promotion, but also how it can exacerbate social ills and precipitate breakdowns in human relationships, aggravated by its public visibility.[51] Building good relationships takes effort and commitment: it can be hard. But SNS are designed to make everything easy, even seeking 'frictionless sharing' at a micro-level without consideration of consequences. The emotional effects of mistakes online can be far from easy to take and might not go away quickly or easily.

SNS generally lack guidelines on how to behave responsibly or on the quality of the human relationships that are created and nurtured through them. This is strange given that those responsible for the early development of Internet-based communications (at a time when there was less online capital) were mindful of the need for special care in this context. They even drew up guidelines for *netiquette*:

> In general, rules of common courtesy for interaction with people should be in force for any situation and on the Internet it's doubly important

where, for example, body language and tone of voice must be inferred.[52]

Whilst the small number of early users, mainly professionals, were disposed to observing and passing on these rules, such observances largely disappeared with the subsequent explosive growth of services and the instant access they offered. Software companies became generally more geared to rapid system implementation. Ethical considerations tended to revolve around aggregated information and the associated system issues of data security and privacy. Whilst such privacy considerations are essential they have, to a large extent, displaced concerns about netiquette, which was prominent in early online communications.

Aggregate notions of 'social capital' have become dominant, strongly reflected in large-scale Internet-based services, which have been characterised more by impersonal paradigms, such as 'network effect', than sensitivity to personal qualities. The weakness of such notions has been exposed in inconclusive findings, seldom showing clear indications of sustained satisfaction being linked with their use.[53] Stronger definitions are needed.

We maintain that a proper definition for humanity should take account of intention and agency. This immediately brings to the fore the ethical value and material consequences of *karma*: aspiring to *virtuous* actions which are quantified as *puñña* (meritorious deeds), and avoiding non-virtuous actions that are *pāpa* (misdeeds). Social capital in this sense is to be built up by practising moral virtue and this needs to be supported at the outset in the systems architecture.

Buddhist architectures for sustainability

We need to make Internet ethics explicit. From a Buddhist perspective this means incorporating individual motivations, cognitive perceptions and interrelatedness. It may sound preachy, but showing more respect paves the way for greater mutual enrichment and, by extension, more vibrant online communities. Teachings in the Pali canon show how this might be done.[54]

One major factor in the problem of well-being is inadequate consideration of *friendship* – what it really means and how best to nurture it. SNS have generally persisted with deploying a single connection type, labelling it 'friend', a limited and atomistic view that effectively dilutes relationships to their lowest common denominator, enriched only in part by privacy options. Some so-called 'friends' are acquaintances, and some are even unknown to the user. In this scenario, describing relationships is reduced merely to 'friends', 'friends of friends', 'close friends', and so on, resulting in a flattened landscape. Moreover, such a connection can be made instantly, prompting further questions about the value of such 'friendship'.

The Buddhist view is that the right kind of friendship is essential to well-being in society. The Buddha used the term *kalyāṇamittatā*, which means 'association with good friends or good friendship,' and defined it thus:

> Herein, Vyagghapajja, in whatsoever village or market town a householder dwells, he associates, converses, engages in discussions with householders or householders' sons, whether young and highly cultured or old and highly cultured, full of faith, full of virtue, full of charity and full of wisdom. He acts in accordance with the faith of the faithful, with the virtue of the virtuous, with the charity of the charitable and with the wisdom of the wise.[55]

The Buddha expresses in greater detail what this means in the *Sigālovāda Sutta*,[56] which has become a *de facto* code of ethics for lay people, especially for many followers in South-East Asia. In this sutta the Buddha teaches Sigāla, a young householder, about nurturing human relationships as *dyadic* relationships, that is the relationships between two people. He uses a visualisation spanning six quarters or directions – the four cardinal points, plus above and below – according to the type of relationship: parents to the East, spouse and children to the West, teachers to the South, friends and associates to the North, servants and employees to the nadir, ascetics and brahmans to the zenith.

Examining the model more closely, there are six kinds of dyadic relationship:

1. spiritual guide or guru – disciple
2. teacher – student
3. friend or associate (peer relationship)
4. employer – employee
5. spouse (peer relationship)
6. parent – child

A visual depiction using cubes has been provided by Venerable Dattajeevo:[57]

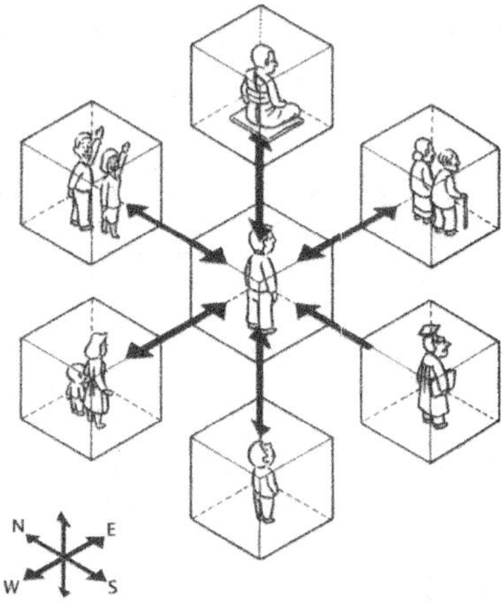

This 3D depiction is strongly suggestive of a tessellation to fill the entire space, which is helpful to indicate our interconnectedness. More usefully, the model also suggests a structural comparison in which the relative strength of the respective SNS architectures may be likened to the distinct properties of diamond and graphite, *allotropes* of carbon – a particularly fitting analogy for carbon-based life forms! Diamond is very tightly packed, with each atom having four strong covalent bonds, spanning 3D in the shape of a tetrahedron. It thus has great hardness or tensile strength (you can't scrape it away). Furthermore these bonds have the same strength in every direction. Graphite, by contrast, is very different, only forming strong bonds in 2D. It has a low measure of hardness and is layered (think of a pencil).[58] By analogy, a relationship going sour in a SNS with just one connection type is like a layer being scraped off graphite, showing its brittle nature, whereas a damaged relationship in a SNS with multiple connection types is more akin to diamond, which remains strong when there is breakage in only one type of bond.

To illustrate further, suppose problems arise at work and are communicated in Facebook among all 'friends'. In this scenario, it would likely be exposed to family, work colleagues, neighbours, and many other types of contacts. On the other hand, an SNS that uses the multi-dimensional architecture would confine the breakage to that particular dimension. Family networks would remain unperturbed and, although weakened, overall stability would still remain. Modelling relationships in multiple dimensions invites us to change our analysis of *social graphs* likewise – to be analysed in at least 3D – and to become far more meaningful. The resilience of a network thus depends on its lattice arrangement, the strength of each bond suggesting the relative importance of *weightings* in the dyadic relationships. Whilst the use of arbitrary groups or 'circles' based on interests is helpful where there is already commonality, it is, as evident from the now defunct Google+, not sufficient, whatever the system of access management.

But is a model drawn from Indian society two and a half millennia ago still relevant today? Well, we still have families, friends, teachers, employers and employees, and many people have spiritual teachers or, if not, confidants, life coaches and psychiatrists. The roles may have shifted somewhat, but the advice, rooted in a universal understanding of what brings human fulfilment, remains broadly applicable. It continues to aid the right view of any activity carried out in society today, including endeavours in science and technology. In particular, it offers insights on viable frameworks for new SNS designs, starting with the *separation of concerns*. Since each connection has its proper place, there is more scope for accepting connection requests and less need to 'unfriend' or drop connections. Such an architecture means parents and children can (and are encouraged to) connect, which some find difficult to do in systems like Facebook.[59] Similarly, this multidimensional model removes the current awkwardness for teachers who receive connection requests from their pupils and struggle with privacy settings.[60] Likewise, when we meet someone at a conference we can classify them appropriately as a business associate.

Having connected, how does one properly nurture a relationship? Again the Buddha points the way: having established the six directions, he instructed Sigāla on how to develop these relationships in a wholesome and fruitful manner, each type having distinct guidance with the focus on the *mode* of interaction (*directed communications* in social media terms). Speech is a major component of these interactions, prompting us to watch out for deception. For instance, false friends are described as those who merely render lip-service, flatter insincerely and so on. Rather, we should aspire to what we may call 'Five Star speech':

> Monks, a statement endowed with five factors is well-spoken, not ill-spoken. It is blameless and unfaulted by knowledgeable people. Which five?

> It is spoken at the right time. It is spoken in truth. It is spoken affectionately. It is spoken beneficially. It is spoken with a mind of good-will.
>
> A statement endowed with these five factors is well-spoken, not ill-spoken. It is blameless and unfaulted by knowledgeable people.[61]

The phrase 'good-will' is particularly significant, being a translation of *mettā*, more commonly rendered as 'loving kindness'. It is pure and untainted in nature: '*Metta* succeeds when it loves, and it fails when it degenerates into worldly affection.'[62] Friendship in the latter context, typical of much SNS use, is often rooted in selfish love or passion, a possessiveness attached to sense pleasure, as distinct from the non-attached *mettā*. The Visuddhimagga describes passion as the 'near enemy' of *mettā*,[63] and thus it is actually an obstacle to building social welfare. The 'far enemy' is hateful speech, spoken with a hateful heart. This is more apt than the simple materialisation 'hate speech', as it is the intention which is most important.

So how does the present crop of social media fare against these criteria with regard to the status update box, a primary organ of communication? The following table shows the typical state of affairs in terms of personal communications:

Vaca Sutta	**Status updates in Facebook, Twitter etc.**
Spoken at the right time	Spoken at any time (and encouraged)
Spoken in truth	May or may not be spoken in truth
Spoken affectionately	May be spoken with or without affection
Spoken beneficially	May or may not be beneficial
Spoken with a mind of good-will	May or may not be spoken with a mind of good-will

A person will likely be more guarded when posting on behalf of an organisation – through *hiri* and *ottappa* – than as an individual at home. Office communication, however, often has its own negative aspect. Personal ambition, office politics and organisational rivalry are all likely to cloud the intentions.

The explicit labelling of relationship types helps us to identify and understand the complexities of their multi-faceted nature. This is a more faithful reflection of society and provides many benefits. For example, it makes it easier to involve parents or guardians in networks, so that they can contribute to the well-being of their children. By making explicit different kinds of relationships they are better contained and the boundaries are clearer. The networks themselves are not just friends of friends (friend networks), but parents of parents (ancestry), teachers of teachers (expert knowledge transfer), and so on in other dimensions, extending outwards, but even across various heterogeneous permutations such as parents of friends. The successive iterations can be scaled up to encompass the human population as a whole within a more meaningful vision of social cohesion, guided by a sound global ethic.

Another key aspect is the cultivation of a relationship over time from the initial invitation onwards. There are other Buddhist teachings that provide guidance here. The *Mangala Sutta* provides 38 blessings, beginning with an injunction to 'avoid fools'. Straightaway we are urged to take care when making any connections.[64] Once connected, we should continue with safeguards; when we first meet someone, perhaps at a conference, we may share just business photographs; but as the acquaintance becomes friendship, the photographs can relate to more personal interests. In a modern commentary on the *Mangala Sutta*, seven levels of association or engagement are described extensively, with parallels for relationships with fools or the wise.[65] Simply making the connection or approach, which in current

SNS would already equate to becoming 'friends', is just the first step. There are six steps beyond that which gradually consolidate the friendship until there is oneness in outlook: making yourself known to them; practising sincerity; being loyal; helping them in times of need; joining up when free to talk and eat together; and then finally a common reflection on the meaning of life (or Dhamma) and getting down to earnest spiritual practice.

How might SNS functionality vary accordingly, in terms of the nature of the functions themselves and features available? Here artificial intelligence can help to distinguish between different stages and provide support at the appropriate level. Connection paradigms can then evolve from the current orientation around possession and acquisition of 'having *x* friends, consuming *y* apps', to dynamic process-oriented relationships whose nature keeps changing and evolving. By supporting these activities, the SNS can serve a healthy role in helping humanity to maintain and strengthen its agency, in conformance with the *Attakārī Sutta.*

6

Ensuring Online Safety

Safety-critical design

THE PRINCIPLES OF the *Sigālovāda Sutta* can revitalise many other approaches to the design of software systems. One aspect, now causing alarm bells to ring, is the hitherto neglected problem of safety, human safety. In candid remarks a number of prominent figures associated with existing systems have admitted deleterious cognitive and emotional effects. Among them, Sean Parker, former President of Facebook, has made reference to a so-called 'dopamine hit'.[66]

In addition to its addictiveness, Parker pointed out that badly designed SNS can exploit 'human vulnerability' in a similar way to malware, by facilitating harmful speech in status updates and accepting 'friend' connections at moments of distraction. The mind weakens when it is pushing outwards and is scattered, whereas it becomes more resilient when it internalises and is focused. Furthermore, it becomes 'cold' if not actively cultivating virtue. It is not just Buddhism that makes such observations. Work by Mary Helen Immordino-Yang and others, in collaborative research between educational psychology and neuroscience, has indicated that the way technologies are used does not provide enough time to reflect and offer compassion, admiration and other noble human virtues. Interviewed for a university news item she states:

> For some kinds of thought, especially moral decision-making about other people's social and psychological situations, we need to allow for adequate time and reflection.[67]

Personal safety becomes prominent with increased exposure to content other people make available. The flip side of 'affordances' that create opportunities for creativity, learning and sharing is an array of misdeeds and misinformation that can deeply harm society. Various kinds of protection are required: against malevolent people; against violations of property; and against inappropriate content. More than ever social protection requires qualities of vigilance and heedfulness. This places an obligation on system designs to be *robust* as far as upholding and protecting wholesome relationships. This means in turn that any implementation delivers what is specified, and does not engage in extra unspecified (and harmful) behaviour. This should be a fundamental architectural requirement of any responsible platform.

The rich structure of the six directions can assist by providing the means for members of the social network to police itself, not in a heavy-handed way, but out of loving-kindness and compassion, where all the protective relationships (such as friends and relations) are properly involved. Society is better protected where these structures are in place and supported.

How might this be realised? Let's first give the notional service a name. We suggest *Sigala*, an allusion to the householder who was instructed by the Buddha; but we change it slightly by making all the vowels short and putting the stress on the 'i' (as in 'Figaro'!)

Now we may proceed to specify system requirements, starting with registration, which we envisage as an entry dialogue to establish legal identity and how one personally identifies oneself. This should be a reflective process, where registrants can determine elements of a persona, perhaps aided by various categories that they can select and rank – such as age, religion, nationality and ethnicity. They can make it multi-faceted, defining their appearance to others dependent on the 'recipient' (type of connection). So from the outset, the new user is made aware of the principle of sharing *selectively*, reducing the chance of strangers accessing sensitive details.

In the case of children, where such discriminatory awareness is crucial, the system can identify the parent (or guardian)–child relationship type as a dependency and authorise the guardian to act as a gatekeeper or moderator. It can start when the guardian registers a minor so as to ensure the right data and permissions are entered. Henceforth they can be kept informed in various ways of how their child is using the network – for example, if a young child wishes to make a connection to someone who is not connected with their guardian or a relative, then the guardian receives notification and might be expected to give permission. We should generally put children at the forefront of design. Ideas could be trialled in some kind of 'tutorial mode', in which we can link to relevant resources at each decision step; we could keep some elements of this scaffolding for children, similar to how Junior Scrabble provides a simplified board to help learn spelling. A playful user interface could enhance the presentation, perhaps supported by the introduction of an AI assistant.

Once registered and using the network, close attention can be given to the status box (and other message areas) with guidance, especially for minors, on entering and posting content. System checks on submission can, as already operating in some networks, usefully deploy AI to help to prevent inappropriate messages and generally target inappropriate patterns of behaviour with warning messages as befits the circumstances. Machine learning alone might struggle to maintain a careful balance between freedom of expression and responsible speech given all the nuances of language, including irony and sarcasm. To make this more human, therefore, community elders who are experienced users of the system should be able to contribute on an ongoing basis to the creation, evaluation and refinement of the guidance that is subsequently implemented in algorithms. The service itself should abide by a code of practice setting out how it will deal with threats and abuse, including clear guidelines on the reporting process.

Safety engineering approaches for human protection

Even with the right ideas for the system architecture, there may well be unanticipated weaknesses in the design, which could be made worse by an implementation developed in the wrong way. It can result in an unsafe product. We therefore need to consider a safety-oriented methodology that can contribute towards its assurance.

So what is *safety*? We may define safety as freedom from harm. In Computer Science the field of *safety-critical systems* commonly defines *safety* as 'protection from critical loss', principally of life. Along similar lines, in society as a whole we may define *safety* as protection from fatality and significant degradation in the quality of human life - not just physical, but emotional and mental as well, extending across the *khandhas*.

In the context of SNS, safety also has an external sense, being protection of one's regard - one's profile and reputation. A SNS should therefore be considered robust only if it offers effective social protection. A system that makes it easy to connect with anyone through a single weak connection is not robust: when an accepted connection goes sour it can cause severe reputational damage. As we have seen, when someone shares information about another person in a harmful way and there is recursively open connectedness, it spreads very rapidly and destroys trust, causing great long-term damage to relationships that have been built over time. It is like a ship with just a single storage compartment; when it gets pierced, it floods throughout and then sinks.

Protection can also be characterised as having two dimensions: *horizontal*, in terms of the separation of concerns into different types of relationships; and *vertical* in terms of depth of relationships. It means that restricting sharing to specific kinds of connections of at least a certain depth will help limit indiscriminate propagation.

The intersection of people's preferences requires additional consideration. When content involving more than one person is shared or tagged, one person may like to tag a photo in a particular way, but not all the people tagged may want the photo to be so widely shared or agree with the choice of tags. The principle operating here can be 'not taking that which is not given' (the second Buddhist precept). An individual can specify their sharing options in terms of each direction, e.g. 'family photos in which I feature only with family' should only be shared among family members. If a family member wants to share this photo more widely then they will be prompted to seek permission from the content creator.

In the same spirit as pure mathematicians wanting assurance for their proofs of theorems, formal methods can help to provide assurance that safety-critical software really is safe. The methods have historically been regarded as specialist and expensive to deploy. For this reason they are generally used to aid reasoning in the early phases of the software lifecycle and often confined to medical, aviation, defence, and other sensitive or heavy-industrial applications. However, the methods and tools have reached a maturity that justify broader scope, especially when the budgets available to tech enterprises are substantial.

So we briefly mention that process algebras, particularly LOTOS, are well-suited to modelling social networks as distributed communication systems. Furthermore, we may use temporal logics (formal systems for reasoning about properties over time) to specify safety properties and check that they are satisfied by a given design or specification. We can therefore determine answers to questions oriented to social protection, such as: Can the system enter a state in which a bad action *X* happens? If bad action *X* happens, can news of it reach person *Y*? Will the system always offer connectivity with trusted friends of connection type *Z*?

Interventions and attention

Parker's psychological point about 'dopamine hits' reflects a deliberate, but unadvertised, purpose. The 'attention economy' has become a means for large organisations to view our use of the Internet and thereby to maximise revenues. Systems are *designed* to retain and nurture our attention, to keep us in front of screens and to steer us in particular directions, usually feeding some form of consumerism.

This is what is intended by *engagement.* More conducive to well-being, however, is its counterpart, *dis*-engagement, the state of rest in which we have real freedom of choice. We can contrast both by exploring a particular facet in design: *intervention.* This word is derived from two Latin words: *inter*, which means 'between' and *venire*, meaning 'to come'. So an intervention is an act of coming between someone on an existing course or path and the continuation of that path. That 'act' could be a natural phenomenon, as in 'bad weather intervened in the rescue operation', but more usually when it involves people, there is some intention behind the intervention with a view to *modifying the outcome.*

There are numerous kinds of interventions or, rather, micro-interventions, in the design of social networking sites. They may seem helpful, but are often intrusive, especially when repeated. Here are a few examples:

- A web page pop-up prompting us to check the site cookies policy or sign up to a newsletter.
- Regular and frequent e-mails reporting selected network updates. Typically, they convey hardly any information and require clicks to their site to see anything useful. Some of these will link to pages requiring a paid subscription.
- Message notifications via e-mail from a particular contact, where replying requires logging into the network.

The main goal behind these designs is to retain and extend the usage of their platforms. It is mission accomplished if each prompt holds on to and retains attention just for a few more moments before the next prompt comes along. Does that matter? What is the human impact in the short term (in immediate mental functioning) and in the long term (in emotional development)? A handful of such prompts is easily dealt with, but what about the cumulative effect of dozens, hundreds, or thousands ... ? Think about the *sankhārā*, the mental formations and habitual tendencies. Whilst the brain can develop ways to cope with the barrage of interventions, there may be unknown effects if it is unable to process the information fully.

So how do we respond constructively? Teaching mindfulness and skilfulness in attending to (and abstinence from) Internet use is a valuable tool that increases our capability and capacity to deal skilfully in such scenarios. But again, just as it's recognised that certain physical environments are not conducive to well-being and merely leaving them as-is is not desirable, the same applies online. We need to identify elements in the design of the online systems themselves that are conducive to supporting such practices and make changes accordingly.

Here we can learn from meditation apps. More than just as add-ons, we should seek to fold in the healthy habits they encourage more universally. How about deploying mindfulness-based interventions to prompt users to take more time for reflection and evaluation? Can we do this especially with a view to the cultivation of moral virtue, which will aid in our personal development and the fostering of healthy relationships? There are already indications from substantial clinical use of Mindfulness Based Cognitive Therapy (MBCT), that such an approach has merit. Whilst not adopting its apparatus, we are encouraged to pay more attention to individual behaviour, and to make choices more skilfully, in a way that genuinely increases our autonomy.

To show how this may be achieved, I am going to apply a teaching method called 'Visible Thinking', a core component of a general technique called 'Thinking Routines' from Harvard's Project Zero, which encourages healthy cognitive habits of observing, questioning and exploring.[68] The first use case is to apply 'Five Star Speech' for status updates, pausing to think before we hit the 'share' button. The five statements lead directly to questions to be presented for what we might dub 'Mindful Thinking Routines' or the 'Thinking Routine for Five Star Speech'.

1. Notice

What is it that you 'see' that prompts you to write? What's inspiring you? How does it make you feel? Is it positive or negative? (These two scenarios correspond to *cāritta* and *vāritta* – wanting to affirm and promote vs wanting to deny or remove.)

2. Think
What do you want to say?
Is it true? Have you got your facts right?
Is it the right time to say it?

3. Imagine
Who's going to read your message?
What will they feel when they read it?
How will it benefit them?

4. Plan
How are you going to say it in the best way? Prompts:
- friendly intentions
- gentleness
(Why do these work?)

On submission, the system can validate the input using machine learning and check particularly for offensive language. If something is flagged as potentially inappropriate, then a further intervention can come into play:

> Did you really mean to say that? It may be regarded as offensive ...

The second use case concerns invitations to connect. Here our Thinking Routines reflect the teachings to Sigāla:

1. **Identify**
   How do I know them? Are they who they say they are?

2. **Think**
   How well do I know them?
   Do I want to associate with them online?

This part could be facilitated by a further Thinking Routine based on other passages in the sutta. For example, with respect to friends, the sutta describes how one should minister to friends and associates (as the North). This can prompt one to ask oneself about what one is ready to give (rather than take).

... Consider
Am I ready to:
(i) be generous?
(ii) show courtesy in speech?
(iii) offer help?
(iv) be impartial?
(v) act with sincerity?

In turn, consider: is the associate a true friend?

... **Imagine** you are in the company of this person. Do they act as follows?
(i) Protect me from being heedless?
(ii) Protect my property if I am heedless?
(iii) Are they someone I can turn to when in danger?

(iv) Are they someone who sticks around when I'm in trouble?
(v) Do they show consideration for my family?

3. Connect!
All OK? Then now is the time to send the invitation. If writing a note of introduction, consider using the Thinking Routine for Five Star Speech.

These kinds of routines are aimed especially at youngsters and are perhaps easier to facilitate in a managed setting. They are designed to redress the absence of many cultural norms in online communications and, thus, to restore greater respect and consideration. It is just a small indication, but hopefully sufficient to intimate a new and safer direction of travel in the design and development of such online services.

7

Are We Here Yet?

THE ACCELERATION IN technological developments has heightened the sense of urgency facing humanity as we hurtle into a future that many feel is getting out of control. The most problematic aspect is that we are becoming desensitised. Whilst much is made of their innovation, these developments are diminishing our critical resources of attention and discriminating awareness, the very properties we need if we are to properly evaluate them. Among the casualties is our understanding of what makes life as a human being truly precious.

To see this more clearly and offer a meaningful response, I started by returning to first principles, with the examination of numbers, which lie at the heart of the mathematics and computation underlying digital systems. Exploring the life and work of their chief exponents, especially Ramanujan, we see how awareness, intuition and creativity are the special ingredients innate to the way humans reveal deep insights. They are all personal and subjective.

Humans possess them irrespective of cultural, ethnic or linguistic background, and they can give rise to beautiful expression. Sometimes in a flash, seemingly out of nowhere.

By contrast, machines have emerged gradually from the strictly intellectual discipline of logic, a rational pursuit that was developed mainly in Europe and North America. Computers interpret series of instructions written in a formal language and are deployed on hardware operating according to observable laws of physics. Like shadows, they can only mimic creativity, typically through a form of randomness.

The distinction is well captured by Pascal's pair of terms, *l'esprit de géométrie* and *l'esprit de finesse*. The former is a way of thinking that proceeds methodically, step by step, like a technician, whereas the latter is proper to someone (like Ramanujan) who sees mathematical properties intrinsic to a situation directly and instantly. The gulf between the two cannot be bridged any more than one can 'square the circle' (the challenge of constructing a square with the same area as a given circle by using only a finite number of steps with compass and straight edge). It has been proven to be impossible because the area of a circle is a multiple of π, a *transcendental number*, where π is the ratio of a circle's circumference to its diameter. Yet it is tempting to think it *is* possible because one can get closer and closer through approximation, especially through software algorithms, which can rapidly accelerate this process.

Likewise, software can sometimes lull people into a similar misapprehension that computers can *think* like humans. Hence the vigorous claims around *artificial intelligence* and machine learning. However, the human mind has unfathomable depth and is capable of going beyond. It has the *general* ability to see and grasp the whole, not just in mathematics, but in any field of endeavour. Let me illustrate this with a challenge, open to humans and machines:

> Compose a poem in the manner of John Donne's *A Valediction Forbidding Mourning* using compass and rule to convey the beauty of Euler's equation, $0 = e^{i\pi} + 1$.
> Hint: start at the origin.

Supply this as input to any existing AI systems and they will not know what to do with it. Any meaningful engagement would require a process that starts with a human who writes some software. This is the origination that Ada Lovelace referred to; any creativity in outputs would be derived from that person, the original author. Of course, you could write some software that would train machines to learn how to tackle a class of problems like this so that future challenges could be received as input and poetry 'crafted' as output, but again the creativity lies with the original programmer(s). Furthermore, it is in itself only a special case of problem setting and would not go far towards the goal of so-called *artificial general intelligence*, a rephrasing among 'strong AI' proponents which effectively concedes that the nature of the human mind is far more extraordinary than the algorithms they have hitherto devised.

As to why and how the human mind has such sublime qualities is an open question. We have observed that the cultivation of mathematical ability requires conscious directed effort, which is essential to any training – whether in sport or personal development. The Buddha made its importance very clear in his teachings on *karma* (intentional actions), which apply to all human activity. He highlighted the qualitative aspects associated with this effort, so that what becomes significant for us is not just performance but the conditions behind that performance and our relationship to them.

For sentient beings, it is intention that fundamentally defines our relationship to any situation. It is the linchpin of causality or, more formally, Dependent Origination. That intention is ethical. There is a wrong and right intention and its evaluation is in terms of its fruits – whether they increase or decrease *dukkha*, a subjective sense of suffering or unsatisfactoriness. This gives rise to a body of teachings on moral virtue as a prerequisite for the development of mind and associated aptitudes. Giving explicit attention to a few basic rules of training provides the groundwork for well-being and human flourishing, and in particular supports the practice of mindfulness, already recognised as an antidote to scattered mental states.

We start to realise what really brings benefit and fulfilment. We find that it is the *quality* of the experience, being fully present, which often arises from very simple things. That attention itself requires nurturing and needs an ethical perspective – the cultivation of heedfulness, which develops sensitivity internally and externally. It is the threefold life of generosity, moral virtue and meditation practice that brings about greater wisdom, and ultimately insight into the nature of reality – a far cry from 'big data'! Such qualities are not readily measurable and don't feature in international well-being indices, but without them there is a drift to mere efficacy.

While humans can in some limited aspects be compared with machines, their 'operation' is radically different. In terms of 'processing', there is more than number crunching in human computation; for a human, a fundamental distinction emerges from the ethical perspective, whereby human processors 'compute' by purifying themselves of defilements, an entirely internal orientation. A key action is inaction – creating the conditions for stillness, the cessation of mental chatter. Stillness allows the mind to transition and sink into deeper levels of mind. In contrast, when a program pauses and a computer's CPU becomes idle, it is doing nothing, nothing gets processed, there are no insights gained, no access to another dimension; it has to *do* something to enter another state.

Another indicator of the difference between humans and machines is the power requirement: for machines, solving challenging problems requires more computing power and hence consumes increasing amounts of energy. However, a moment's inspiration is all it takes for a human to find a novel solution. It might be based on many hours of meditation, but such practice is known to involve reduced breathing and quietening of other physiological functions, so it consumes less power.

We should keep this in mind when faced with positivistic views of digital technology that place the words "improvement" and "optimisation" in close proximity. What kind of *optimisation* do we really need? What is realistically achievable? And what, if anything, are we prepared to give up to attain it? As well as determining the financial costs involved, we need to assess the impact in broader human terms. We should remind ourselves that we are *already* struggling to cope with the everyday technology that *currently* exists.

It may be tempting to leave it to machines to take care of things, to welcome automation for an 'easier lifestyle', but that is actually an act of resignation. And a surrender of agency. It should be a core health requirement to retain and enhance the ability of *all* humans to continue with independent living, able to think, speak and act freely of one's own accord. To protect this right, we need to recognise that the repeated enabling or disabling of basic actions has significant enduring effects. We should guard especially against becoming overly dependent and appreciate that we may not yet have realized our own resources for well-being in body and mind.

A more compelling case for machine learning, with the prospect of being supercharged by quantum computing, emerges from the potential breakthroughs in medical sciences ('Imagine a world where cancer is a thing of the past') and the reduction of social inequality through faster telecommunications. Yet even here the benefits are material and offer no guarantee of mental well-being – we all have to die of something, so might it not be better to channel more resources to prepare us mentally to die peacefully, to help with palliative care?

According to Buddhism, our physical health is dependent upon our mental health and any fruits are subject to conditioning, especially our previous *karma*. This view tends to qualify any medical guarantee with a statement along the lines, 'Whilst we should aim to treat all beings with compassion, the fruits are subject to the individual's *karma*'. There are no guarantees in the human predicament.

For the Buddhist, *optimisation* means enhanced virtuous qualities – greater generosity, loving kindness, patience, etc., the so-called Perfections (*paramis*). All very well, you might say, but what practical guidance is there to help us evaluate the burgeoning technology being thrust upon us? Fortunately, there is a little-known teaching of the Buddha, recorded as the *Attakārī Sutta* (the Self-Doer), which could well provide the critical guidance we need. It comes in the form of a checklist for human agency: autonomy, initiation, effort, exertion, steadfastness, persistence and endeavouring. We simply determine according to each of these in turn what impact a future technological development has for us individually, not just in the immediate instance, but in the long term. For example, a mobile phone would not be considered a boon if its continued use meant our ability to communicate face-to-face gradually became impaired.

Whilst machines don't have the same kind of intelligence as humans, their usefulness as tools offers endless possibilities that even extend to the study of Buddhist literature. They may, for example, formalise the language in which Buddhist texts are recorded and hence help to clarify their meaning, making choices in interpretation more apparent. We have seen how this can be done for processes, which are inherent in both computing and Buddhism, modelling aspects of Dependent Origination using process algebra.

This is only intellectual reasoning. In no way does it really bring direct insight. Moreover, there is an important observation to be made with this particular example. In the interplay of sentient life and inanimate machines there is a temptation to describe them alike as merely processes which are constantly changing, nothing more. This may be coupled with a view that the Buddha taught flatly 'there is no self', which leans towards annihilationism. It weakens the case for human beings to survive and strengthens the case for transhumanism, the interfacing and merging of human and machine. Yet the Buddha did not teach an unequivocal 'no self' doctrine that many assert, but rather pointed to what was subject to change and therefore *not* self and what therefore should be let go of for the *lokuttara dhamma* (the transcendent state, *nirvana*). Hence, to speak of 'co-existence of machines and humans' is to accord machines an inappropriate status that threatens not only human autonomy but also human potential; we should never discount the subjective qualities of awareness and intuition that are essential to who we are.

Most practical applications of software algorithms

concern consumer activities. Does Buddhism have anything to say in this sphere? About the extent we should trust them to help with what to buy? Concerning today's to do list? Or even what social causes to support and who to vote for?

We have seen that Buddhism is especially relevant as it casts light on problems concerning definitions of *well-being*. For the Buddha well-being was an easeful subjective quality of sublime serenity; at the social level this means self-sufficiency and authenticity of genuine interpersonal relationships. Getting to the heart of the problem, the Buddha addressed social well-being in teachings on friendship that he gave to a householder called Sigāla. He described how to discern genuine friendship from fake friendship, how to cultivate different kinds of relationships – kinship and non-kinship – and how to do so authentically and sustainably. From this perspective, we see how the waters have been muddied by the notion of 'social capital', a form of collective materialism which is typically expressed in the literature as an 'aggregation of resources'. They are evaluated in terms of the buzz of network activities and the possession of loosely termed 'friend' connections, which lead to evaluation by numbers.

Simply by lumping all relationships together as being of one type, these networks have often become a source of considerable dissatisfaction almost since the day they were launched. We don't have to continue with these diminished notions for we have shown how we can apply the Buddha's teachings to structure more meaningful connections and furthermore how to develop them carefully, especially with regard to essential elements of communication. Next time you enter a message in the status box consider: is it true, expressed with good intent, in a friendly tone, beneficial, and is it the right time? Is it, in short, 'Five Star speech'?

The Buddha was adept at turning things around: he would take existing Vedic practices and use the same framework, but completely repurpose it. We can do likewise. If the core design concept is *intervention*, which so far has been slipped in to diminish cognitive function and foster addiction, we can flip this round, so as to design interventions to recover and strengthen cognitive abilities. By adopting the Harvard Thinking Routines, we have shown how a more humane system can be designed without difficulty. It may mean less online activity in terms of quantity, but that activity will be more conscious, more intended, and more meaningful.

All told, there is certainly the potential for human flourishing in the digital sphere, but it will only happen when we understand how consciousness is conditioned and shift the ethical basis from material things (phenomena and data) to behaviour (intention and action). Only then will we be able to recover the present moment.

> Mindfulness. Breathe in, knowing that you are breathing in ... breathe out, knowing that you are breathing out ...

Epilogue

THIS BOOK WAS almost finished; only the Epilogue remained. Then Covid-19 arrived.

The virus and its ramifications have been profoundly disturbing, but have they really changed us and our behaviour? If so, how? What has been the contribution of digital technology and what might we usefully learn from the pandemic?

The severity of this coronavirus has forced us to realise what is essential in terms of the physical sustenance we need to live (food, shelter, exercise) and what is a nicety. It has also cast into high relief the critical importance of other people: how our social welfare has depended on and been nurtured not only by continued associations with our family, friends and neighbours, but also by the unexpected kindness of strangers, often prompting reflection on services we previously took for granted.

We have also had to face a third element: ourselves. Something has changed. It is intangible but profound. We have had to learn how to become more self-sufficient, to know what it is to be ourselves without the usual social props. The lockdown around the world

– staying at home in confinement – has afforded most of us time to slow things down, and to make fundamental decisions about what we really value. It has been an opportunity to abandon wasteful activities, to become more mindful of what is essential and also more sensitive to the needs of others, an invitation to act through compassion.

The predicament and the response at various levels have taken their toll. Primary attention has been given to the physical disease, but support for people's mental well-being has been relatively neglected, leading to a build-up of stress, considerable frustration and a polarisation of opinion – not only on how the situation has been handled, but on social affairs more generally. It has been extensively affected by social media, which has aggravated rather than reconciled differences.

In view of its profound and far-reaching impact on humanity, our experience of this global pandemic is helping to shape how we move ahead. When we eventually emerge from these troubling times, we will enter another period, perhaps even more critical because it will set the tone for future generations. Do we continue with deeper and more meaningful reflection and sharing, or do we regress to a state of selfish distraction and materialism, where we become increasingly antagonistic and polarised? Are we really satisfied that we are designing and using technology in the right way in light of these challenges?

The coronavirus pandemic – as an emergency and opportunity – thus gives more urgency to the issues that we have raised in this book, especially concerning well-being and the development of nuanced and sustainable relationships rooted in authentic friendship. These help us to sharpen our focus on the role of technological development vis-à-vis human and humane development.

For example, it has been proposed that a majority of the population need to use smartphone apps that provide continual 'monitoring' of essential life signs and that this requires ever-faster and even more dense global networks. Once again, artificial intelligence (or machine learning) is advocated as a core means of enhancing life prospects. Is it really necessary? Who is doing the monitoring, for whom and for what purposes? What consideration has been given to viable alternatives? Once again, we must insist on asking questions about intention and agency.

Is AI part of the solution or part of the problem? If it keeps progressing then where will it lead? At the moment, the outcome lies in our hands, for – as we have argued at length – we know and recognise that the spark of creativity rests with *us*. However, certain perspectives concerning 'strong AI', regarded as fringe just a couple of decades ago, have been rapidly gaining prominence (and commercial interest). That is why we need robust terms of evaluation, as expressed in the *Attakārī Sutta*, and we *all* need to take part.

The ultimate super computer already exists. It is not merely physical. It covers form, feelings, perception, mental formations and even consciousness. What might that be? Samsara! Samsara, the continual round of becoming, is a kind of psycho-physical machine. In a way it is the complete social credit solution – a fair reward and punishment system, with realms of luxury and deprivation computed as a result of our *karma*. But it is also an endless dystopia as nothing lasts, the environment keeps changing and we don't have control over it.

The Buddha saw the futility of this eternal round, prompting his search to properly understand and then transcend it. A sense of independence and freedom are fundamental to the human quest, to any aspiration to disentangle ourselves and go beyond the confused state of affairs:

> As a deer unbound in the forest goes off to whatever pastures it wishes, so a wise person, looking out for freedom, should live alone like a rhinoceros.[69]

Whether we live alone or in a large household we can all benefit from clearing the right mental space. This will enable us to be mindful and have clear comprehension, so that we are better placed to control technology wisely rather than find ourselves being witlessly controlled by technology. Our evaluation must be astute and it must be constant.

Technology needs to reach greater maturity. In earlier chapters I introduced the Sigala project for sustainable social networking, whose software architecture is based on the Buddha's teachings. It provides novel structuring elements to nurture robust and sustainable relationships of many kinds, including heterogeneous networks.

To help keep the designs fluid, the design process may be likened to a sculptor working on a maquette. It is an ambitious project and would surely benefit from many voices to refine that maquette; it needs a team. So if you are interested in these ideas, may I invite you to explore the project website, http://siga.la/. It may be just the beginning of a wonderful new journey that will take us beyond our present confines and a little closer to the peace and well-being we all desire.

Notes

1 Obituary – Freda Newth Wint, Amaravati Buddhist Monastery, 7 December 2015, www.amaravati.org/obituary-freda-newth-wint/
2 Helen Joyce, *Natural Born Mathematicians,* December 2001, https://plus.maths.org/content/os/issue19/features/butterworth/index
3 *Pensées de M. Pascal sur la religion et sur quelques autres sujets* (Guillaume Desprez, Paris, 1670)
4 *Illuminating India: 5000 Years of Science and Innovation*, Science Museum, London, 4 October 2017–22 April 2018, www.sciencemuseum.org.uk/what-was-on/illuminating-india
5 Carol Clark, 'Mathematicians Find "Magic Key" to Drive Ramanujan's Taxi-Cab Number', eScienceCommons, Emory University, 14 October 2015, http://esciencecommons.blogspot.com/2015/10/mathematicians-find-magic-key-to-drive.html
6 S.R. Ranganathan, *Ramanujan – The Man and The Mathematician,* Great Thinkers of India Series (Asia Publishing House, Bombay, 1967)
7 N4: Intellect and Intuition, *ibid.*
8 N44: The Task of Proving, *ibid.*
9 Marianne Freiberger, 'Pure Maths in Crisis?', *Plus Magazine*, 19 March 2019, https://plus.maths.org/content/pure-maths-crisis
10 Semir Zeki, John Paul Romanya, Dionigi M.T. Benincasa, and Michael F. Atiyah, 'The Experience of Mathematical Beauty and its Neural Correlates', Frontiers in Human Neuroscience, 13 February 2014, www.frontiersin.org/articles/10.3389/fnhum.2014.00068/full
11 Ken Ono in T.V. Venkateswaran, 'Relevance of Srinivasa Ramanujan – The Man Who Knew Infinity', *India Science Wire, The Hindu Business Line*, 22 December 2017, www.

thehindubusinessline.com/news/science/relevance-of-srinivasa-ramanujan-the-man-who-knew-infinity/article10000537.ece

12 It has been eloquently argued by Richard Gombrich that Pali was the language actually used by the Buddha. Richard Gombrich, *Buddhism and Pali* (Mud Pie Books, 2018)

13 For most spellings I choose the Pali form, but *karma*, the Sanskrit form, is so well-known that it is natural to adopt it.

14 *Yamakavagga: Pairs*, Dhp1-2.

15 *Lakkhaṇa Sutta: The Marks of a Great Man*, DN 30

16 For a concise introduction to Buddhist ethics, applied to many current issues, see Damien Keown's *Buddhist Ethics: A Very Short Introduction* (Oxford University Press, 2006)

17 *Upajjhatthana Sutta: Subjects for Contemplation*, AN 5:57

18 *Attakārī Sutta: The Self-Doer*, AN 6.38 (PTS: A iii 337).

19 *Samaññaphala Sutta: The Fruits of the Contemplative Life*, DN 2

20 *Declaration towards a Global Ethic*, Parliament of the World Religions, Chicago, USA, 4 September 1993, https://www.global-ethic.org/declaration-toward-a-global-ethic/

21 Surveys of US and UK households have shown that despite increased material prosperity (consumer choice) severe social problems remain. Avner Offer. *The Challenge of Affluence: Self-Control and Well-Being in the United States and Britain Since 1950* (Oxford University Press, 2006).

22 Bhikkhu Bodhi, *The Guardians of the World* (Buddhist Publication Society, Kandy, 1993), www.accesstoinsight.org/lib/authors/bodhi/bps-essay_23.html

23 Paul Trafford, *Avoiding Pamāda: An Analysis of the Fifth Precept as Social Protection in Contemporary Contexts with Reference to the Early Buddhist Teachings* (Dissertation, M.St. Study of Religions, 2009), www.academia.edu/34976455/

24 Allan G. Bromley, 'Charles Babbage's Analytical Engine, 1838', Annals of the History of Computing, Vol. 4(3), 196–217 (1982).

25 Note G *in* Richard and John Taylor, *Sketch of the Analytical Engine Invented by Charles Babbage, Esq.* (1843), reproduced online at www.fourmilab.ch/babbage/sketch.html

26 Note A, *ibid.*

27 Alan Turing, 'On Computable Numbers, with an Application to the Entscheidungsproblem', Proceedings of the London

Mathematical Society, 2, Vol. 42(1), 230–265 (1937), https://londmathsoc.onlinelibrary.wiley.com/doi/abs/10.1112/plms/s2-42.1.230

28 Taylor, Note G.

29 Ada Lovelace, Journal entry for 5 Jan 1841, Lovelace Papers, Bodleian Library, Oxford University, 175, folio 199.

30 Alan Turing, 'Computing Machinery and Intelligence', *Mind* Vol. 49, 433–460 (1950), www.csee.umbc.edu/courses/471/papers/turing.pdf

31 J. McCarthy, M.L. Minsky, N. Rochester, C.E. Shannon, 'Proposal for the Dartmouth Summer Research Project on Artificial Intelligence' (Dartmouth College, 1955), https://250.dartmouth.edu/highlights/artificial-intelligence-ai-coined-dartmouth

32 Roger Penrose, *Shadows of the Mind: A Search for the Missing Science of Consciousness* (Oxford University Press, 1994)

33 Celeste Biever, 'Inside the Mind of an Autistic Savant', *New Scientist: Life*, 30 December 2008, www.newscientist.com/article/mg20126881-800-inside-the-mind-of-an-autistic-savant/

34 *Kalama Sutta,* AN 3.66

35 As advocated in Cal Newport, *Digital Minimalism: On Living Better with Less Technology* (Penguin Random House, 2019)

36 *Nibbāna Sutta: Parinibbāna,* Udāna 8.3

37 The *khandhas* are much discussed in the suttas, with a whole book devoted to them in the Samyutta Nikāya. For an introduction, see a study guide by Thanissaro Bhikkhu, www.accesstoinsight.org/lib/study/khandha.html

38 See e.g. *Cūḷasuññata Sutta: The Shorter Discourse on Emptiness,* MN 121

39 *Rohitassa Sutta (To Rohitassa),* AN 4.45

40 Rocco de Nicola, 'A Gentle Introduction to Process Algebras' (Notes), IMT – Institute for Advanced Studies Lucca, 2014. https://pdfs.semanticscholar.org/12d9/eae1638729aeb237b5be445ee91ecdd3c5d7.pdf

41 ISO 8807:1989, *Information Processing Systems – Open Systems Interconnection – LOTOS – A Formal Description Technique Based on the Temporal Ordering of Observational Behaviour* (International Standards Organisation, Geneva), www.iso.org/iso/catalogue_detail.htm?csnumber=16258

42 *Paticca-samuppada-vibhanga Sutta: Analysis of Dependent Co-arising*, SN 12.2
43 Thanissaro Bhikkhu (trans.), *Chachakka Sutta: Sutta on Six Sets of Six Bases*, MN 148, https://www.accesstoinsight.org/tipitaka/mn/mn.148.than.html
44 Bhikkhu Vimalaramsi, an experienced meditation teacher, emphasises reading out suttas in full. See 'The Read Out-Loud/Memorization Sutta Project', Dhammasukha Meditation Center, https://library.dhammasukha.org/read-aloudmemorise.html
45 I.B. Horner, 'Attā and Anattā', *Studies in Comparative Religion* Vol. 7(1) (1973), www.studiesincomparativereligion.com/Public/articles/Atta_and_Anatta.aspx
46 *Mahāparinibbāṇa Sutta: Last Days of the Buddha.* DN 16
47 This literal interpretation is taught in meditation programmes of the Dhammakaya tradition, such as those offered by the Middle Way Meditation Institute, https://mmipeace.org
48 J.F. Helliwell and R.D. Putnam, 'The Social Context of Well-Being', Philosophical Transactions of the Royal Society London: Biological Sciences, Vol. 359, 1435–1446 (2004)
49 A. Portes, 'Social Capital: Its Origins and Applications in Modern Sociology', Annual Review of Sociology, Vol. 24, 1–24 (1998)
50 P. Bourdieu, *Le capital social: notes provisoires.* Actes de la Recherche en Sciences Sociales. L'École des hautes études en sciences sociales, 1980
51 D. Miller, '"Fas" Book (Facebook) in Trinidad', *Material World* blog post, New York University, 7 February 2010, www.materialworldblog.com/2010/02/fas-book-facebook-in-trinidad/
52 S. Hambridge, 'Netiquette Guidelines. Network Working Group Request for Comments: 1855' (Internet Engineering Task Force, 1995), http://tools.ietf.org/html/rfc1855
53 Esteban Ortiz-Ospina, 'Are Facebook and Other Social Media Platforms Bad for Our Well-Being?' (Our World in Data, Global Change Data Lab, UK) https://ourworldindata.org/social-media-wellbeing
54 Many of the ideas expressed here were first presented in 'Supporting Kalyāṇamittatā Online: New Architectures for Sustainable Social Networking', 3rd World Conference on

Buddhism and Science, Mahidol University, 2010, http://siga.la/pubs/2010/WCBS_Trafford_socialnetworks.pdf

55 *Dīghajāṇu Sutta: Conditions of Welfare*, AN 8.54

56 *Sigālovāda Sutta*, DN 31

57 Bhikkhu P. Dattajeevo, *Man's Personal Transformation* (trans. A. Methmanus) (Dhammakaya Foundation, Bangkok, 2005), p.206

58 'Diamond Graphite', Miles Mineral Museum, Eastern New Mexico University, www.enmu.edu/about/general-information/local-events-and-info/arts-and-culture/miles-mineral-museum/diamond-graphite

59 Jimmy Smallwood, 'Facebook: Should Parents "Friend" their Children?', BBC Radio 5 live, BBC News Magazine, 10 December 2010, www.bbc.co.uk/news/magazine-11968954

60 Jean Mackenzie, 'Schools Need Rules for Teachers on Facebook, Union Says', BBC: Newsbeat, 10 February 2011, www.bbc.co.uk/newsbeat/12417183

61 *Vaca Sutta: On Appropriate Speech*, AN 5.198

62 Acharya Buddharakkhita, *Metta: The Philosophy and Practice of Universal Love*, WH 365,6 (Buddhist Publication Society, Kandy, 1989), www.accesstoinsight.org/lib/authors/buddharakkhita/wheel365.html

63 Vsm. IX.98

64 *Mangala Sutta: Blessings*, Khp 5

65 *A Manual of Peace: 38 Steps Towards Enlightened Living* (Dhammakaya Foundation, Bangkok, 2005) pp.31–32, 44

66 Mike Allen, 'Sean Parker Unloads on Facebook: "God Only Knows What it's Doing to Our Children's Brains"', Axios, 9 November 2017, www.axios.com/sean-parker-unloads-on-facebook-god-only-knows-what-its-doing-to-our-childrens-brains-1513306792-f855e7b4-4e99-4d60-8d51-2775559c2671.html

67 Carl Marziali, 'Nobler Instincts Take Time', USC News Science/Technology 14 April 2009, http://uscnews.usc.edu/science_technology/nobler_instincts_take_time.html

68 'Visible Thinking', Project Zero, Harvard Graduate School of Education, www.pz.harvard.edu/projects/visible-thinking

69 Bhikkhu Bodhi (trans.), *Khaggavisāṇa Sutta: The Rhinoceros*, Sn 3

Acknowledgements

I would like to thank Damien Keown and Kate Norrie for kindly reading and providing comments on early drafts of this work. I am also grateful to Tony Morris for the considerable care and attention he has shown throughout.

About the Author

Paul Trafford lives in Oxford. He holds postgraduate degrees in mathematics, computer science and the study of religion, and has spent most of his working life in higher education and museums, mainly in the field of IT.

Paul received Dhamma transmission from his mother, the late Fuengsin Trafford, who developed her Buddhist practice at Wat Paknam Bhasicharoen monastery in Thonburi, Bangkok.

He has served as Buddhist Faith Advisor for the University of Derby and as Trustee of the International Interfaith Centre in Oxford. He was also a founding Director of the Dhammakaya International Society of the UK.

He blogs at: https://paultrafford.blogspot.com

Printed in Great Britain
by Amazon

44838601R00078